Bastide on Religion

The Invention of Candomblé

Key Thinkers in the Study of Religion

Edited by Steven Engler, Mount Royal College, Canada

Key Thinkers in the Study of Religion is a series of compact introductions to the life and work of major figures in the study of religion. Each volume provides up-to-date critical evaluations of the place and value of a single scholar's work, in a manner both accessible to students and useful for instructors. Each volume includes a brief biography, analyses of key works, evaluations of criticisms and of overall impact on the field, and discussions of the work of later scholars who have appropriated or extended each key thinker's approach. Critical engagement with each key thinker's major works makes each volume a useful companion for the study of these important sources in the field. Aimed at the undergraduate and introductory graduate classrooms, the series aims to encapsulate and evaluate foundational contributions to the academic study of religion.

This series is sponsored by, supported by the North American Association for the Study of Religion (NAASR), an affiliate of the International Association for the History of Religions.

Published:

Bourdieu on Religion: Imposing Faith and Legitimacy
Terry Rey

Levi-Strauss on Religion: The Structuring Mind
Paul-François Tremlett

Forthcoming:

Dumont on Religion: Difference, Comparison, Transgression
Ivan Strenski

Derrida on Religion: Thinker of Differance
Dawne McCance

Rudolf Otto on Religion
Gregory D. Alles

Bastide on Religion

The Invention of Candomblé

Michel Despland

Routledge
Taylor & Francis Group
LONDON AND NEW YORK

First published 2008 by Equinox, an imprint of Acumen

Published 2014 by Routledge
2 Park Square, Milton Park, Abingdon, Oxon OX14 4RN
711 Third Avenue, New York, NY 10017, USA

Routledge is an imprint of the Taylor & Francis Group, an informa business

British Library Cataloguing-in-Publication Data
A catalogue record for this book is available from the British Library.

Library of Congress Cataloging-in-Publication Data

Despland, Michel.

Bastide on Religion: The Invention of Candomblé / Michel Despland.
p. cm. — (Key thinkers in the study of religion)
Includes bibliographical references and index.

ISBN-13: 978-1-84553-365-6 (hb)
ISBN-13: 978-1-84553-366-3 (pbk.)

1. Bastide, Roger, 1898-1974. 2. Religion. 3. Candomblé (Religion)
4. Bahia (Brazil : State)—Religious life and customs. I. Title.

BL2592.C35D47 2008
306.6092—dc22

2008001912

Edited and typeset by Queenston Publishing, Hamilton, Canada

Contents

Table of Thematic Boxes

It is not worthwhile to go round the world to count the cats in Zanzibar.

Thoreau, Walden

Preface

Doughnut stands in Indonesia offer wildly coloured doughnuts: green, red, pink and yellow. The multinational companies in search of global markets adapt their product to local taste; with lots of food coloring, they emulate the brightness of tropical spices and vegetables that accompany the traditional dish of rice. This is called glocalization. The statistics compiled by the Canadian Government invite individuals to indicate, if they want, their ethnic origin (with guarantees of privacy). The public has just been informed that in a few years, the majority of the population will be ethnically hyphenated. Instead of English and French, there will be answers like Irish-Polish and French-Chileans. Muslim immigrants in Canada have started arguing for Fridays off. In Islam, Friday is not a sabbath; the religious obligation is to attend Friday prayer which takes an hour or so of the individual's life. But Muslims having noticed that Christians and Jews cannot be forced to work on Sundays or Saturdays, they want for themselves what the Unions obtained for the others. Their militancy is proof their assimilation to Canadian ways.

These three examples are instances of what is technically called acculturation. Studies in areas where cultures come in contact have multiplied exponentially in the second half of the twentieth century. The contact is sometimes peaceful, sometimes viciously conflictual, with many intermediate possibilities. The cultures exposed to each other often have unequal powers. The religious factor often looms large. In all cases, each side is affected by the other, and countless forms of hybridation appear. Even if there are stable barriers, clear rules and only a modest amount of interaction, each side looks at the other and this suffices to launch internal processes in the individuals belonging to the two cultures thus exposed.

Roger Bastide, French sociologist (1898–1974) was an important and early player in this rapidly developing field of inquiries. His intellectual life soared in 1936 when he became professor of sociology at the University of São Paulo in Brazil. Beside his professional interests, he was very alert to modern literary trends and he quickly attuned himself to the local cultural effervescence. Brazil was turning away from its dependence on

European high culture and some highly educated Brazilians were getting keenly sensitive to the artistic creativity among the lower strata of their society.

Brazil had imported more African slaves than any other American country. In 1938, sixty years after emancipation, there were forms of racial prejudice. There were also sharp class distinctions, great wealth and extreme poverty, crime and violent outbursts. But there was also a variety of religious movements and, above all, Brazilian musical and artistic style. Today t-shirts are worn proclaiming "A third Portuguese, a third Indian, a third African, 100% Brazilian." Bastide was intrigued by what was, in his eyes, an entirely new mix of old and familiar factors. So he embarked upon a range of studies on the Afro-Brazilian religion vibrant in the Northeast, especially in Salvador de Bahia. He examined what happened to African gods when they were immigrants in a new land. He also looked at the social and religious transformations from the conditions of the old sugar plantations to new ones in the industrialized south. Quickly he became a contributor to another newly emerging international field of interests: African religion in the Americas.

When he returned to end his career in Paris, he became acquainted with a new generation of anthropologists who had done fieldwork in Africa under the conditions of de-colonization and were paying sharp attention to the transformation in the old rituals and to the rise of new sects. He worked with the UNESCO establishment and its denunciation of racism. He became a major actor in the worldwide studies of the phenomena of acculturation and de-culturation that were then being undertaken. With many colleagues, he saw very well the ineptness of many dominant theories of economic development, which thought they could remain ignorant of local cultural factors.

His life and work are thus part of a shift among French social scientists toward a passionate ethnology in the era of de-colonization. Religious cults, rituals and associations matter; they change under stresses and their struggles are an integral part of the groups struggles to shape some future for themselves.

Michel Despland
November 18, 2008

Acknowledgements

My thanks go to Steven Engler (São Paulo) who invited me to São Paolo instructed me in things Brazilian and gave me a chance to see something of what I had read; to Ivan Khan (Toronto) and Jennifer Reid (Farmington) who gave most useful bibliographical tips; and to Marie Paule Martel-Reny (Montréal) who did precious work on the text. I am also much indebted to the bibliography prepared by Claude Ravelet and available at http://www.unicaen.fr/lasar/bastidiana/BIO-BIBLIO.html

Chapter 1

An intellectual biography

Roger Bastide (Nîmes, 1898–Paris, 1974) accepted the labels of sociologist, anthropologist and ethnologist. All are appropriate, but only in part. First because Bastide was trained as a philosopher and never lost sight of the large questions philosophers try to handle. A second point is that his sensitivity to human beings nearly always shone through any label that he wore or received. Thus Bastide was also a writer—and one who reflected on the work that writers and other artists do. But scholars are necessarily localized—we do our jobs in a modern specialized world—so a sociologist he shall be, adding however that sociology, for him, included anthropology and ethnology.

His Ph.D. equivalent was an *aggrégation en philosophie* obtained in Bordeaux in 1920, where he followed the teaching of Gaston Richard, who was a pupil of Émile Durkheim (and his successor in the philosophy chair of Bordeaux). His early intellectual context places him in the second generation of Durkheimian sociology. He reached his intellectual maturity in Brazil, during his professorship in sociology at the University of São Paulo, from 1938 to 1954. He showed there the scope of his interests and pursued his now classical work on Afro-Brazilian religions. From 1954 to the year of his death, his outreach was international, centered in Paris. His scholarship flowered in the era of the cold war and the rise of the civil rights movement in the United States. But the general context in his own life was rather the era of post-colonialism. Post-modernism was not yet in the air; although it can be argued that the ground was being laid for it.

Bastide was raised in a protestant family and was educated in the schools of the Third Republic, which were *laïques*, meaning that religious affiliations and ideas were ignored. It will be necessary to pay some attention to the characteristically French approach to the study of religion, as it was shaped by the institutions of a State that practiced strict separation between itself and the Church.

The plan of this book is simple: it follows a chronological sequence, with three thematic final chapters. There is a reason for such a plan. To build the edifice of science is a cumulative affair and young minds learn by becoming acquainted with what their predecessors did. But no architect ever drew the plan for the overall edifice and scholars, even beginners, do more than follow specifications when they cut their stones. It is hard to imagine a building in which the foundations keep being remade and the ground floor plan revised—and in which odd-shaped bricks are made to fit. Yet this is in fact what happens. Scholars in the field of religion are historical beings who think and write about other historical beings. No fresh mind merely takes up the task where others left it. Each, in some sense, starts all over again. To draw attention to this reality I attempt in this book the intellectual biography of a man who started all over again.

This book is, in the end, a case study in the invention of a religion. Candomblé existed before Bastide wrote about it, just like America existed before Columbus discovered it. But Bastide and Columbus put what they

Morale laïque

In 1882 the government of the newly established Third Republic abolished the compulsory teaching of Catholic catechism in public schools and replaced it by a course in "secular morality." But to translate "*laïc*" with "secular" is misleading. The *morale laïque* was based on rational considerations and excluded evidences from any revelation, but it had, at first, a theistic basis. The idea that God was the source of the moral law was very much part of it. (The programme was elaborated by a group of civil servants among whom Protestants of Kantian allegiance were over-represented.)

Laïcité in France is a public philosophy and a moral stance. Teachers are supposed to do the job of the nation, not of any community, and are expected to keep their religious opinions to themselves in the classroom. This ethos is strong and was accepted by all Protestants and Jews, a significant proportion of Catholics and of course all anti-clericals. Thus self-restraint is widely accepted. For instance teachers in the public schools ordinarily refrain from wearing jewellery indicating their religious allegiance when they exercise their official function in public spaces. (The recent legislation against pupils wearing ostentatious religious symbols, such as Muslim headscarves, was in line with custom).

In 1905 a similar political coalition passed laws imposing a strict separation between Church and State. This law in 1918 went as far as prohibiting any religious symbolism on public monuments to the war dead. (Yet at the beginning of the Great War, a chaplaincy corps—Catholic, Protestant, Jewish—was instituted in the army for ministries of individual succour and consolation). To sum up, laïcité is a philosophy of the State, not a social process.

found on the map. The peoples of the Americas knew the land existed before 1492, but those who did not (or not yet) live on this Continent found out about America only after the work of what we may call, using a somewhat archaic sense of the word, their inventors. Of Bastide's three books on Candomblé, the first was published in Portuguese and the other two in French. All three became quickly available in both languages and the third and most weighty one was promptly translated into English.[1]

Chapter 2

Breaking the glass and striking the rock

The early career of Roger Bastide was the predictable one of a graduate of the *aggrégation de philosophie*: he taught in the senior years of a sequence of provincial colleges. One of his earliest available texts is an address to the award-winning 1926 graduates in Lorient (Britanny). His topic was regionalism and tradition and this leads him, as the genre requires, to direct exhortation.

His choice of topic, we can see now, and what he did say are indicative of life-long concerns. It was also rooted in crucial debates of the decade in France. It has been noted that from the end of the nineteenth century, memory became a central topic for a whole range of authors: psychologists, historians, philosophers—and novelists. Suffice to mention two monumental works: *Matter and Memory* (1896) in which Henri Bergson developed a contrast fundamental to his whole subsequent work, and *Remembrance of Things Past* by Marcel Proust (1913–1927).[1] The issue of memory became socially and politically important because of the notion of tradition. Solidarity and tradition were at the core of the agenda of early sociology on France. That the individual is born into a pre-existing social whole and subsequently shaped by it was the basic premise that led to fertile inquiries. Traditionalism however, quickly became the rallying point of political anti-modernity movements (first led by persistent royalists and staunch Catholics). In the 1920s the defence of tradition and regionalism became monopolized by newly energized, post-war, right-wing bellicose movements that extolled rural wisdom and the memory of the soil from which the dead speak. (Maurice Barrés had orchestrated this theme in his novels).[2]

Bastide approaches the issue of regionalism from the other end of the political spectrum, from a firmly republican outlook. But he does not name it so—and generally avoids loaded ideological terms. He simply affirms that the simple joys of maintaining tradition are exhausted. The young, he adds, do not expect anything from warmed over, left over remains of the past, and dusty regional museums.[3] He draws his examples from the region of his birth, the Cévennes and Languedoc, and from that of his students, Britanny. These are two contrasting parts of France, each with strong regional folklore and identity: South and Northwest, sheep and cows, olive oil and butter. Both are also heartlands of durable, contrasted confessional identification, protestant and catholic.[4] He stresses that before they were placed on clothes-horses behind showcases in museums, the folkloric dresses and bonnets of Arles and of Brittany were not petrified. When worn by living women, they were varied and they changed. Strong winds, he concludes, come from the past and fill our sails, but we steer our boats—at least we want to, and rightly so. It is a crime against the "durability of provincial feeling" to protect it from the future in apparent safety behind a window, and with a little dish of repellent to keep the insects away. So Bastide calls for a new aesthetics.[5] What is beautiful is much more than just what is classical and lasts.

Forty-seven years later, in 1973, on another formal occasion, Bastide delivers an address in Geneva, "Le sacré sauvage," in which he affirms at the outset that "the instituted gods" are dead. After decades of ethnographic studies of, and proximity with, "archaic" societies, he multiplies examples of "savage trances" from distant continents and notes the appearance of similar phenomena in the Europe of the 1960s. And he concludes with a metaphor from the Bible, a text he knew from childhood. The old man invites his listeners to see in the unskilled experiences of the youthful discoverers of festive communions and alternative lifestyles, nothing less than imitations of Moses. The Hebrew leader, he reminds his listeners, struck the rock of Horeb with his rod, to make water stream from it so that the people in the desert could drink.[6] The psychoanalytic echo is explicitly acknowledged but is not allowed to exhaust the intended meaning. When individuals are offered numerous pale substitutes to religion by consumerism and therapies, fresh and live meanings are born in countercultural movements, and fling an important challenge to all organized religions. This was to be his last major speech.

Chapter 3

Symbols, memory and anticipation: Sociology from Durkheim to Gurvitch

The uncontested leader of the sociological school in France in 1900 was Émile Durkheim. Three aspects of his work are of concern to us here.

Durkheim was first of all determined to make sociology a science. His models of science were, like those of his generation, drawn from the natural sciences; hence his slogan about treating social facts as things, the search for "elementary forms" of religious life, and the recourse to stable morphologies. Durkheim also maintained a sharp differentiation between his sociology and psychology, a discipline recently admitted to the holy shrine of approved methodical sciences.[1] This led naturally to his opposition to any of the nascent forms of psychology of religion, which all seemed to him to eschew the only possible rational explanation of religion, namely the sociological. The translation in 1906 of William James *The Varieties of Religious Experience*[2] did not receive much attention in the group of the *Année sociologique*.

Secondly, the societies he knew and which nourished his reflection were what we might call societies that considered themselves complete. France and Germany believed they had evolved into a classical form and seemed both determined and able to go on as they were, colonial expansion being the only ambition left for the future. Thus he was not inclined to study evolution and social change but rather the mechanisms of stability in societies that had evolved toward their apparent end-goal.

Thirdly, Durkheim thought that sociology held the key to a proper moral education for the public schools. We shall have to return later to his notion of the *morale de la République* and his understanding of the goals of the *école laïque*. For now let us turn to the first issue.

We saw that it was Gaston Richard who guided Roger Bastide in his study of sociology. Richard was a contemporary of Durkheim and can be

Émile Durkheim (1856–1917)

The son of a rabbi, Durkheim quickly ascended the steps of the French educational system and published two doctoral dissertations, one on *The Division of Labour* and one (in Latin) on the political thought of Montesquieu. He read the nineteenth century social thinkers with zeal. With a professorship in Bordeaux (in philosophy) he taught and published on social solidarity and education. His studies *The Rules of the Sociological Method* (1895) and *Suicide* (1897) established him as a strong voice in the nascent discipline of sociology. From 1898 he directed an annual publication, l'*Année sociologique,* which gathered the work of a number of authors, mainly his students, and included numerous book reviews. In 1902, he moved to Paris. In 1912 came *The Elementary Forms of Religious Life: A Study in Religious Sociology* (translated 1915).

Durkheim promoted a scientific approach determined to treat social facts as if they were things. He documented the impact on the individual of collective consciousness. By insisting on seeing social realities as external to the individual, he was criticized for being an anti-individualist. Yet in ethics, law and politics, he was a staunch defender of the rights of the individual.

counted among his disciples; he certainly enjoyed the support of the master to succeed him in Bordeaux, and he managed to get the designation of his chair changed from philosophy to social science.[3] But Richard was to cut an independent path. He showed interest in gender studies, a then uncharacteristic interest among Durkheimians.[4] But above all he criticized Durkheim on the issue of his interpretation of religion, which he considered dogmatic. As a matter of fact there are grounds to believe that he objected to the strongly self-assured manner of the teacher known as *the boss* in his circle. "Let us beware of sociological metaphors," he wrote;[5] he might have added a warning against making of "society" the subject of a sentence and thereby tending to make of it an agent. Thus he shared the general unease with Durkheim's "social realism" that was found outside the circle of early sociologists. He flatly challenged the sociologist's case for sociology being the only rational approach to religion and rejected the alternative "God or society."[6] The short formula "God is society" was also unacceptable under the form "society is God." The article "Dogmatic atheism in the sociology of religion" (published in 1923, six years after Durkheim's death) reviews the founder's books and discusses other interpretations of "primitive religion." It strongly opposes the identification of religion with forms of constraint.[7]

The article critical of Durkheim was published in a Strasbourg journal, the *Revue d'histoire et de philosophie religieuse*. It is relevant to know that the journal had a Protestant affiliation. (In 1905, the date of the laws separating Church and State, Strasbourg was German and therefore unaffected; it keeps to this day two confessional university Faculties of Theology). It should also be known that Richard became a Protestant at age twenty. There is a pattern here. The cause of psychology of religion and the objective of studying religious experience were supported by many protestant university professors, most visible among them being Raoul Allier. It seems that these French scholars, with their sensitivity to individual conscience and their feeling that ecclesiastical authority was not necessarily oppressive (and certainly was not in their own church), were, as a rule, uneasy about the polarized opposition between reason and religion. An institutional battle was lost by this group in 1907 when the candidacy of Allier to a chair in the Collège de France failed, sociologists

Religious studies in French universities

In 1879 the Government of the Republic instituted a chair in the history of religion at the prestigious *Collège de France*, a center of higher learning which does not grant degrees. In 1886, in the course of a programme of reform, the Goverment closed down the faculties of theology (Catholic and Protestant) in the universities. They went on doing their work as privately supported institutions (now with equal public support for the individual students). The money made available was devoted to the opening of a section in "*sciences religieuses*" in the École Pratique des Hautes Études, a newly funded institution of higher learning in Paris. This section promptly became a centre for the history of religions and social sciences of religion, and still is.

There was also a plan to open chairs in history of religions in the various Faculties of Arts but few were established. (Religious strife and rivalry among disciplines is usually given as the reason). Erudition on religion flourishes in France, but it is distributed across disciplines (history, sociology, anthropology, ethnology) and area studies. So the fact that Bastide's entire career occurred in places that had no specialized focus on religion is entirely normal.

What suffers from this situation is what is now known as theory of religion. Some philosophers work on philosophies of religion, some of great merit, but they ordinarily know little concrete religious material and, if any history of religion, only the Western history. There being little or no teaching of basic history of religions in the universities, the currently acknowledged need to give information on religions in the public schools suffers from lack of adequate training programmes. Now, it is the Québec Ministry of Education that leads in the Francophone world in the planning of suitable programmes on religious culture for public schools.

reaching the ear of the cabinet minister and thereby managing to confirm their practical "scientific" monopoly.[8] After leaving Bordeaux, Bastide kept a correspondence with Richard and with Allier.[9]

It is hardly surprising therefore that Bastide's first book is entitled *Les problèmes de la vie mystique* (*Problems of Mystical Life*).[10] In 214 pages the author reviews the recent (and abundant) literature on the subject. Catholics had produced a few great and respected monographs on mystical saints[11] and psychologists had observed and measured (and sometimes provoked) mental and physical states that break from ordinary courses of consciousness. Bastide finds both types of study wanting: the testimonies of the saints are ultimately used as evidence for some version of Christian theology and the doctors study only the pathological. But he pays attention to the account mystics give of their experiences. He declares himself ready to use all existing methods to explore this complex matter but refuses to judge on any ultimate theological matters. A verbal account of experience is always something social, and uses terms culled from the cultural and theological context. When, for instance, he examines the writings of Saint Theresa, his goal is description rather than explanation; he also notices the strength of the public actions that followed her contemplation. He counters the pathologists with the advice of William James (which in fact goes back to Jesus): judge oddities of behaviour by their fruit and not by the ascribed causes. He therefore can add a historical judgement: in Christian history mysticism is more ascetic than orgiastic, more an active discipline than a passive surrender. He also distinguishes between minor mystics or mystics of imitation, and the major ones who are, in general, creators of a new self and attempt a complete systematization of life. Mysticism is to him a pursuit of knowledge and a method of life. It uses tradition in an original manner. There is then one key conclusion: mysticism is not a state but a dynamism.

The book is kept in print. It is a clear and balanced review of the literature then available. Two easy ways are carefully avoided: that of classifying some behaviour and some types of thinking as abnormal or pathological, and that of using "experience" to turn the wheels of some theological mill.

A couple of articles of the same period confirm the intellectual focus Bastide is in the process of elaborating: it remains attentive to both psychology and history. In 1931 "Un mysticisme sans dieux" explores a variety of disciplined attempts to empty oneself of one's own being to arrive at a stage of knowledge through "conaturality" with what is known. He argues such paths are present in a variety of cultures, and most clear in the context of religious systems. They can all be developed by education.[12] Perhaps even more significant is the 1934 article "Dieu et la Révolution: Essai sur les rapports entre l'Église et la démocratie." In it Bastide gathers evidence to show that Christianity in nineteenth century France was not just what French people in 1934 call "a religion." It was in fact a movement of thought that was deeply involved in struggles for emancipation and change; it did not act through Church authorities but through some famous writers and major actors on the social and political scenes. In other words, the modern division of segments of society that confines religion to "religious institutions" cannot do justice to the dynamics of nineteenth century French history. He pointedly advises socialists not to lose sight of the religious sources of their movement.[13] Bastide was sounding a highly original note at the time when matters of public concern were not to be tainted by religious considerations. These articles were first published in a magazine for the general public.

A second book confirms both the mastery of topics and the clear focus of the young author. *Éléments de sociologie religieuse* (1935)[14] begins with a definition of object, limits and methods. Religious feeling is human before it is social, but it develops only when shared. Durkheim's disciples err when they confuse the religious with the collective. Bastide's sociology has modest goals: to examine collective religious facts, and carefully leave aside deeper problems of knowledge (and theories about the nature and scope of the human mind). Facts will be gathered from comparative history of religion and ethnography (in the perspectives of the then emerging school of cultural history). The recourse to a wide variety of material from the history of religions, which includes religions of more civilized people, is in itself a departure from the habits of the early Durkheim group who looked mainly at people they called primitive. (Was it to keep things simple?).[15] Four parts examine in turn the sphere of the sacred (and differentiate religion from magic), the social elements of religion, the religious systems, and views on the origin and evolution of religion. The conclusion argues that social determinisms create the objects of sociology but social processes have unpredictable beginnings and promise new and unfamiliar sequels. "The sociology of religion can observe their presence but it cannot explain them." In two hundred pages, the author reviews the available literature, summarizes positions and states his own. The book was recently translated and published as *Social Origins of Religion*. The foreword presents it as a work of transition in the history of French sociology and lauds it for its broad perspective.[16] The publication has not created much excitement among scholars in the English-speaking world. I would still recommend it to first year students and advise them to wait a year before moving on to Foucault or Baudrillard.

And now to the issue of morality. Durkheim did not fail to notice that in his day religion was losing its power to shape behaviour. And, perhaps more keenly than many, he felt the need to find a successor and thus offered the services of his nascent sociology. Note that in the 1880s the young Third Republic took the teaching of Catholicism out of the public schools and put in its place the teaching of a *morale laïque*, which rested largely on the ethics of Kant as interpreted by mandarins in the civil service. Hence Durkheim's life-long interest in the practices and philosophies of education and his writings on morality, where he, again, wanted to put forward the scientific, i.e. sociological, point of view and ensure it prevailed.

Durkheim's great public occasion as teacher of moral ideals came during the Dreyfus Affair. A military trial had hastily found the Jewish captain guilty of treason. Little by little intellectuals appealed to public opinion to obtain a retrial since the first one had a strong appearance of being a miscarriage of justice. Ferdinand Brunetière, who spoke with the prestige of a member of the French Academy and director of the great *Revue des deux mondes*, wrote in derision of the "intellectuals" who claimed to have a conscience and who loudly asked for a revision of the trial. Brunetière's underlying theme was the evils of modern "individualism." Contemporary intellectuals, he said, put their reason above authority. The distinguished author claimed to locate here a large and urgent social and political problem: individuals err in thinking that the rights of the individual take precedence over alleged social needs. In reply Durkheim wrote a defence of Dreyfus and his supporters. But he also joined the intellectual issue: he makes individualism into a social idealism. It is the social product that will ensure morality in the new society. The human person is considered as sacred "in what one might call the ritual sense of the word." There is no reason of State that can contest the autonomy of reason, freedom of thought and the cult of man.[17]

Steven Lukes showed that Durkheim's thinking on morality "operated at a number of different levels" and, in the end, coped with philosophical questions he did not grasp well and failed to resolve. At the time of his death, Durkheim left papers for a book that was to come to terms with the issue. In his effort to show how society could provide a genuine ethics, he moved from studies of constraints to consideration of ideals, looked more closely at the problem of representations, moved away from the reliance on morphologies that characterized his earlier work and began to develop a theory of symbolism.[18] But on one point he did not waver: his commitment to the hegemony of science included the claim that norms can be derived from facts. The scientist *knows* and therefore can prescribe.[19]

Caught in the ruts of the debates on *morale laïque* suitable for the republican public school that was sharpened after 1905 by the new laws on separation of Church and State, Durkheim's view on morality came under frequent attack. Leaving aside the predictable views of the apologists of organized religion, one should, to help locate Bastide, focus on the writings of Gaston Richard who seems to have spoken for many. He found in the *patron* of sociologists "an illegitimate slide from the social fact of solidarity to a principle of moral obligation, from social pressures to moral rules, and in particular from the fact of organic solidarity to the demands of justice". (This is Lukes' summary.)[20] Richard also explained that from the first he felt that Durkheim completely ignored the problem of moral evil. (The last work Richard published in his lifetime was one on sociology and theodicy).[21]

Richard spoke for many. A vague dissatisfaction on the issue of society and ethics was rampant after World War I, when it appeared that victory and peace had not solved all problems. An important treatment of some of the issues appeared in 1925 in Halbwachs' epoch-making study on *Les cadres sociaux de la mémoire.*[22] Durkheim had staked his hopes for a good society under modern condition in an increasing specialization of functions. To the "mechanical solidarity" of traditional societies he opposed the organic one of societies practicing the division of labour.[23] Halbwachs however, argues that the members of the modern working class, unlike the aristocrats of old, tend to become confounded with their task, even, at times, in their own eyes. He adds that work has become a matter of techniques, so that no room is left for the exercise of personal qualities, for improvization and initiative.[24] He notes, almost in passing, that members of the modern working class have little knowledge of their past, and that their collective memory has become impoverished. Is the modern working class culturally deprived? Thus he draws attention to the crucial importance of the phenomena of memory, the place where history and psychology meet. Thereby he takes sociological inquiry into what is perhaps the most personal, if not intimate, part of the individual's life. With this new interest in memory, individual and social, religious phenomena are no longer the one area where sociology and psychology come to some overlap. The stakes for the life of a culture are high in Halbwachs' eyes. The loss of class memories among the workers is very much to their social and political detriment.[25] This issue is a very good gate to enter into the interpretation of Afro-Brazilian religion put forward by Bastide and we will return to it.

So Halbwachs argues that moderns are too absorbed in their specialized tasks. To resist this sort of captivity they should strive to remain in touch with genuine humanity in free social exchanges, where opinions and sentiments become freely expressed in non-professional ways. His examples are taken from the life in the salons of the elite, and this makes his argument sound quainter to our ears than it should.[26] Halbwachs saw that Durkheim's vaunted modern organic solidarity was rather mechanical. (We would certainly also agree that the traditional societies Durkheim called mechanical are more organic). Halbwachs also refers to the pages of Weber on the Protestant ethic—as was common in his day he limits their relevance to "anglo-saxon societies"—but criticizes the rationalization it commends as being an illusory bearer of progress.[27] Halbwachs moral solution in these 1925 pages may seem to us rather weak, but we must include him in the list of early antecedents to the post-modern critics of techno-bureaucracies and alienation through working conditions, even when they are profitable.[28]

The generation of sociologists that came after Durkheim thus opened a general agenda on the processes whereby societies reproduce themselves. Births ensure only an ongoing demographic basis (and not always an adequate one in the eyes of elite opinion). What gets transmitted across generations? What do the young do with the world into which they were born and which a series of authorities explained to them? What sort of memories do they keep? What if anything do they learn from the memories of their parents and grand parents? What traditions do they feel inclined to maintain? How do they interpret what they bring from their childhood to their adulthood? We will see that this is part of the general sociological agenda that Bastide took to his study of transported African slaves and of Afro-Brazilian religions.

In 1924, Marcel Mauss, Durkheim's nephew, introduced a new topic to the sociological menu. Addressing a group of psychologists, he called on them for more collaboration and drew to their attention the phenomenon of *attente,* commonly translated as "expectation." By asking for a look at human attitudes toward the future, he invited his listeners to consider societies as being not finished and merely striving to last, but also as stirred by diverse imaginations of their future. He thus added a second chapter to the consideration of the problems inherent in the human experience of temporality, which had begun to be explored through the phenomena of memory and the problem of tradition. He launches inquiries into the sociology of expectation (a field that can be nourished by abundant data from messianic movements), and adds another chapter to the sociology of religion, which, in 1973, Henri Desroche was to label the sociology of hope.[29]

The same year, 1925, saw another break with the Durkheimian orthodoxy that had important methodological implications. Marcel Mauss, prudent innovator, moves away from the notion that everything social is obligatory or a source of obligation. He turns his attention to the freer kinds of social interactions.[30] He also launches the notion of total social fact on its successful career. He argues that the tendency (inherited from the scholastic psychology of faculties) to divide up human realities into various segments must be curbed. Physiological, mental and social factors enter jointly into the construction of behaviour. Abstractions are useful but tend to be too rigid. What is concrete and alive is whole. His 1925 essay identified one such "total fact" and began what is still an ongoing exploration of its numerous ramifications: the practice of giving. He drew attention to what he called the threefold obligation of giving, accepting and returning the gift. The *Essai sur le don*[31] orients the sociological mind toward observation of what we might call micro-bonding between individuals and between groups, and to the reality of soft moral obligations. This opens a path for theories of the origin of customary social bonds—when society gels—other than the foundational effervescence Durkheim featured as the basis of his version of totemism. Mauss extends his observation of gift practices in archaic societies to tentative conclusions on modern economics, politics and morality: wealth is not just for consuming, but also for giving and thereby governing.[32] We err in thinking that moderns are dominated by an ethics of merchants: aristocratic largesse and liberality in expense are not dead in the commercial world, since they remain a source of prestige. The study of concrete realities will, he thinks, confirm his basic rule that in society humans must either trust or distrust each other. This is the point where ethics begins, because trust and distrust are at the basis of practises of inclusion and exclusion. The matter of trust and distrust is thus also a point ethics never leaves behind. Civility and its rich range of soft obligations become key notions Mauss gives to sociologists and ethicists to ponder.[33] The study of representations and the analysis of the social impact of symbols, and of the dynamics of their daily use, receive at this point a much fruitful extension.[34] Durkheim limited himself to the study of religious rituals to explore collective representations. Mauss invited anthropologists to study the whole range of symbolic exchange.[35] A new agenda is created for the sociology of religion: it is not just the great foundational rituals that are a source of stable meaning; meaning gets shared—and sometimes stabilized, out of the most humble, daily social interaction. The epistemology of the social sciences has to be re-thought.

Richard, Halbwachs and Mauss all reflect in their way the anxiety about the shape their country would take after the blood bath of the World War I. (Nathan Schlanger aptly called this war "the field work in modernity"[36]). Victory had not brought all that it seemed to promise when war was started and fought. There was indeed a post-war quest for a way out of a commonly felt impasse. A traditionalist rightwing opinion, now finally reconciled with the Republican ideology, was bellicose ("make Germany pay"). It was opposed by a variety of pacifist and socialist ideals.[37] The old professional narrowness of the university professors yielded somewhat under the pressure of perceived new problems and the broadening of the agenda. Some sociologists kept accepting the label but wanted to work on a broader science of man. Halbwachs, like Mauss, wanted, for instance, to free economics from nineteenth century theories. In this new context, the sociology of religion became a topic of intense intellectual relevance. The ethnologists who were launching then the work of their lifetime had for what was called religious phenomena, even the most distant ones, the same cool but eager curiosity they showed for all human manifestations. What happens in religious life was placed in the broader context of the rise and fall of symbols and the daily social context of symbolic exchanges. An exhausted positivism that claimed scientific mastery of facts and their laws was yielding to a new view: one of the characteristics of social facts is their symbolic aspect. Dolphins speak dolphin—and never get caught in misunderstanding. Human beings do not speak human; they communicate with each other through what is called "natural languages" namely through the arbitrary symbols used in a group.

Such is the context of Bastide's early adulthood. But to this array of new social and moral explorations and socialist commitment,[38] Bastide adds an element that is uniquely his own, his literary savvy. He read André Gide, Marcel Proust, François Mauriac and Pierre Jean Jouve.[39] In what became the famous "Quarrel of the poplar" Gide had taken on Barrès and the Catholic traditionalists by poking fun at their usual comparison of humans to trees, who prosper by drawing nourishment from their roots. On Gide's views, poplars deplete the land they grow on; being a skilled gardener, he counterposed the example of leeks, which need to be transplanted to achieve a proper growth.[40] Bastide frequented the Parisian literary avant-garde and early surrealist circles. (Some distance away from the outlook of his family!) He published a few poems but fairly quickly settled his voice in the genre of the essay. Some were distinctly literary. They nevertheless showed a difference. His early pieces on Proust, Gide and Mauriac are explorations of the impact of their belonging to different religious families: Judaism, Protestantism and Catholicism. His topic is not the presence or absence of the beliefs characteristic of these groups but—and this move is then highly original—the echoes of their religious affiliation in their sensibilities and way of seeing the world. The three authors are thus treated as free and creative artists who had been and might still be meaningfully exposed to a religious tradition and might have their language shaped by their links to a religious community.[41]

Marcel Mauss (1872–1950)

Nephew of Durkheim, Marcel Mauss first contributed to the enterprise of the *Année sociologique,* in which he published two major studies co-authored with the more historically minded Henri Hubert, “Essai sur la nature et la fonction du sacrifice” (1898–1889) and *Esquisse d’une théorie générale de la magie* (1902–1903). He obtained a position in the Religious Studies Section of the École pratique des Hautes Études and learned a lot from Sylvain Lévi, specialist in Hinduism. After the war (and the death of his uncle), he kept the *Année sociologique* going. Little by little he went beyond the positions defended by Durkheim, most notably the idea that the social facts meet the self as a constraint or coercion. He inclined more and more toward anthropological studies.

His epoch-making 1925 study *The Gift: The form and reason for exchange in archaic societies* shows individuals freely initiating and contracting social bonds. It also demonstrated the value of his determination to study the total man, namely actions that implicate the whole person. He had already pursued this approach in his pages on expectation in a 1924 address to psychologists: expectation (*attente*) implies physiology, psychology and society. In 1934 he opened up another new area of inquiry with the essay “Les techniques du corps.” In 1938 he wrestled with problems of perennial interest with his essay *A category of the human mind: the notion of the person; the notion of self.* A Western cultural tradition of more than two millennia has imprinted on us an implicit notion of person, and this affects our way of seeing others— and our ways of attempting to change ourselves.

His work can be seen as the most sustained effort to understand the nature of the symbolic in all its ramifications in human living. In his last years he tried to map out a version of non-Bolshevik socialism. As Paris was occupied by the Nazis, he resigned from his position as Head of the Section on Religious Sciences in the École Pratique des Hautes Études.

His interest in this area led him to a polemic against an author who had affirmed that Protestantism is totally incapable of nourishing religious art. A first article covered all the texts in Calvin about the Incarnation, the dignity of the body, the place of beauty in human life and the legitimacy of visual arts as long as they remain short of offering images of the deity. A further two articles, “Études d’esthétique protestante” and “Littérature et protestantisme,” give the result of a survey he made in literary circles. The results show that Protestants are frequently caricatured in French literary circles. The most common stereotype about them is their alleged rigid moralism and their disembodied spirituality of the soul. He also finds that opinion in their churches are not very supportive of their writers, and that these excel in novels rather than poetry.[42]

Another article of the same period entitled, *La plongée ténébreuse,* takes the readers into a very different province of the imagination. It uses the Freudian and the Bergsonian "mythologies" to take his readers on two different of excursions into the night world of sleep and dreams.[43] The suggestions of unfamiliar meanings, the half-hidden personal emotions and the wildly unpredictable turns of thought can also be coolly examined and quietly written by this scholar. They are indicative of the broadening of the intellectual agenda that the more gifted moralists and social scientists were led to explore between the two world wars.

There is one more element to be added to the portrait of the young sociologist. The young Bastide read Halbwachs and Mauss (and referred to them in his mature work) but the major impact on his thinking as sociologist clearly was his near contemporary Georges Gurvitch (1894–1965). Born and educated in Russia, Gurvitch had participated in the Soviet Revolution—he could include in his Sorbonne lectures references to what he had said to Lenin—but, disagreeing with the turn the Revolution was taking, left his country in 1920. After a sojourn in Germany where he familiarized himself with the thought of Husserl and with phenomenology, he settled in France in 1925 where he published *L'idée du droit social* in 1930 and *Essais de sociologie* in 1938. The Second World War saw him briefly in New York at the New School for Social Research.[44]

In 1940, when he was already settled in Brazil, Bastide published a substantial article on the sociology of Gurvitch.[45] The article first points out that Gurvitch began as a philosopher, as an expert on Fichte and his doctrine of the will. From the phenomenological school Gurvitch drew the notion that "experience" is a vulgar construction, a reflection of reality, not a direct grasp of pure data. Then Bastide shows how the Russian exile, having worked on the theory of law, began to give a central place to the insight that society is made of layers. (Note that Freud had previously compared the psyche to the Rome of the archaeologists, a pile of remains deposited by subsequent centuries). To this emerging science of diversified mores, Gurvitch adds a voluntaristic ethic, which he calls radically empirical. (William James had given much earlier currency to the phrase "radical empiricism").[46] Like Weber, he turns to the qualitative study of social types, and rallies to a pluralistic (rather than monistic) view of society. He does not expect too much from statistics; instead of laws, he identifies regularities.

Gurvitch found seven superimposed layers in social reality. Bastide summarizes them in this way:

1. On the surface, individuals and things, the demographic and geographical bases.

2. Just below, the symbols used daily for exchange and communication.
3. The social organizations with the varying degrees of pressure they exercise on individuals.
4. Social habits, rites and traditions (sometimes in conflict with level 3).
5. Revolutions, wars and crises that break traditions and innovate.
6. Below it all, the world of ideas and values from which all five levels derive motivating engines.
7. The collective consciousness that lives within and experiments with the spiritual world found in level 6.

Radical Empiricism

At the end of his life William James wrote a series of essays on metaphysical and epistemological matters, which were published in a book under the title *Essays in Radical Empiricism* (1912). British Empiricism considers experience to be our access to reality; Radical Empiricism focuses on the reality of experience. The social scientists work within the first tradition, when they frame hypothesis and seek empirical verification. John Wild has shown that Radical Empiricism has kinship with the European phenomenological tradition. "We have no access to any idea that is necessarily real, nor to any brute fact that is necessarily meaningful" (Wild 1969, 333). The pragmatic view of truth starts from the recognition that there are some things that persistently resist us. The challenge that our minds may enable us to face is the use of our cognitive and other capabilities in order to survive experience. Thus experience is from the ground up subject to positive or negative evaluation. James therefore "warns the empiricist against confusing the objective perspective of the natural sciences with the wider and richer horizon of the life world" (Wild 1969, 299). Concrete thinking, which locates us in the life world, is always existentially first in the mental flux. On this view, religion is to be considered as "a man's total reaction upon life" (Wild 1969, 294–300). "Knowing is nothing more nor less than a particular kind of relationship within the flow of experience" (Taylor 1996, xv).

James wrote an essay on "The experience of activity." "Whenever we had successfully lived through an activity situation, we should have to be permitted, without provoking contradiction, to say that we had been really been active, that we had met real resistance and had really prevailed" (James 1958, 167).

Gurvitch spoke of radical empiricism to point to the existential fact of voluntary acts and attitudes. Bastide shows in the rise of Afro-Brazilian religions an example of concrete thinking striving in harsh circumstances to keep human life human, and ready for the continuation of experience.

Gurvitch stresses that micro-sociology shows individuals open to each other, while macro-sociology shows them bound to each other without inter-personal communication. Bastide concludes that Gurvitch effected a profound transformation of tendencies in French sociology by stressing the variety of sociabilities and brought this about by drawing from what is best in the German sociological schools.[47] It is commonly acknowledged that Gurvitch turned a page on the Durkheimian heritage by ceasing to systematically oppose individuals and society. He found little use for the general view of religion as an ingredient in the general theory of society. Gurvitch inserted religion deeply in all the various layers of society and thus called for attention to its diversified forms. In the 1950s he also developed the notion of a multiplicity of social times to which we shall have to return since it shows a convergence with what Bastide was writing in the years after his return to Paris.[48]

Gurvitch was notorious in Paris for having a difficult character. We might say, more politely, that he was impatient of intellectual mediocrity. But he

Max Weber (1864–1920)

Son of a liberal parliamentarian in Berlin, Max Weber started with an interest in economics and law and explored historical matters such as: how did the West achieve a high degree of economic rationality and why? This led him to investigations in sociology of religion. His most famous work, *The Protestant Ethic and the Spirit of Capitalism* (1904–1905, translated 1930), showed how the transformation of religious anxiety brought about by Protestantism in its Calvinist forms led to a sense of vocation, a new inner-worldly form of asceticism, and that this contributed to the creation and rise of capitalism. Against Marxists he had identified a case where ideas had social consequences.

His sociology from then on focuses on meaningful action and slowly extends itself to a comparative study of civilizations. He came to see religions as ways of coping with the problem of theodicy, namely of evil and undeserved suffering. ("The social psychology of world religions" 1922–23). He thus published studies on religion and society in China, in India and, most importantly in ancient Israel where he saw the beginning of a disenchantment of the world under the auspices of monotheism.

The work of his later years focussed on the problems of political sociology, and developed the concepts of leadership, domination and bureaucracy. He cast the rise of the modern State in dark terms. His last two essays "Science as Vocation" and "Politics as Vocation" end up drawing a stark contrast between the rigorously objective and value-free commitment of science and the need of power politics to promote and combat gods.

His enduring contribution is the focus on meaningful action and the development of ideal types that permit us to group and understand the multiple forms of human realities.

opened the clearest avenues of thought that led to the French elaboration of the sociology of knowledge.[49] In the eyes of many of his contemporaries, the sociology of knowledge his views made possible, remained considered as the foggiest part of the social sciences.[50] The air cleared somewhat when it became accepted that sociologists are part of society too. It also helped to realize that science is what scientists do. Bastide worked happily with Gurvitch in his *Laboratoire de sociologie de la connaissance* at the Sorbonne upon his return from Brazil. The 1940 article, I think, can be considered as indicating the solidly acquired sociological base on which he was to build his original (and now classical) Brazilian work and his subsequent investigations.

We should then consider Bastide as doing his own work from within the general matrix of post-Durkheimian sociology. Durkheim's work on social categories and primitive forms of classification was being recast in a radical way. Original views were slowly taking shape: social categories are employed in different ways in different levels of society. The new input from ethnologists and anthropologists made it clear that "natives" are fellow human beings and not just "living fossils" that are of interest only to scientists who care to know what we evolved out of.

On this last issue a major confrontation had arisen between Durkheim and his colleague and friend Lucien Lévy-Brühl. The latter, originally trained as a philosopher, stressed the break between primitive categories and the rise of modern science but kept trying to figure out, on empirical bases, where exactly the difference was to be found.

All sociologists of the second generation agree that Lévy-Brühl was the winner in the debate with Durkheim. Thus Lévy-Brühl made a crucial contribution to the new explorations of the issues involved in cultural change, cultural transmission and cultural contacts. It was admitted that moderns both share common mental features with the so-called primitives and have acquired new, reflective, methodical rational capabilities. The problem remains of what is to be done with the uneasy balance between these two kinds of mental functioning. (Some romantic views began again to extol the ways of the primitives). I alluded already to a whole generation of ethnologists: they went to their fields after profiting from such advances. Claude Lévi-Strauss is the obvious intellectual giant in that group. In turn, even historians rallied to the view that, within the same civilization, mentalities change through the centuries. So it became commonly acknowledged that to know human beings in their fully historical dimensions, scholars need to make a detour, to look also at many other human beings, and, most probably, at some living in very distant and very different societies.

Lucien Lévy-Brühl (1857–1939)

After brilliant studies in philosophy and evidence of intellectual gifts in many areas, Lévy-Brühl was appointed to the Sorbonne to teach the history of modern philosophy. His friendship with Durkheim led him to look into the sociology of mores, and this led to his book *Ethics and Moral Science* (1903), in which we can see the hinge between the two periods of his intellectual achievements. By 1910 he had focussed on what was to be his dominant interest for the rest of his life and published *How Natives Think*. Primitives do not reason badly; they think differently from us. He found in them what he called "the law of participation": things can be at the same time themselves and something else. Thus natives do not ferret out contradictions with anything like our usual zeal. His formulations led Evans-Pritchard, Cazeneuve and others to credit him with the discovery of "residues", that is, that there is an irrational part in the very structure of social behaviour. (The term "residue" was first used by Pareto to point to aspects of economic patterns that cannot be accounted for by rationality or reasonableness).

The reception of his work gave him occasions to travel (notably in South America), meet ethnologists and intensify his readings. Five other books tried to get right the crucial matter of "participation." He gave up his early notion of "pre-logical thought." He kept looking for intermediaries between primitive and civilized mentality, and pondered the various cultural ways in which cognitive elements become detached from affective factors. He does not seem to have ever been able to entirely agree with himself. One affirmation remained constant: our modes of cognition separate the subject from its object too much. At the time of his death, he left notebooks that were published by his friend Maurice Leenhardt and are commonly considered to be his best work.

In 1925 he created the *Institut d'Ethnologie,* thereby enshrining a name for the new science at the time when in the United States the designation of anthropology gained currency. He asked Mauss to be the secretary of it. He then resigned his position as professor of philosophy to have time to pursue his now dominant intellectual interests, try to forge appropriate language for getting hold of the facts and keep provoking questions to which he did not find answers. He made it necessary for epistemologically alert social scientists to pay attention to what ethnologists were finding out in their field work. He accredited the notion of the co-existence in our minds of two levels of mental habits.

Leenhardt draws attention to his "discovering a freedom of thought in the experience of reality," and to his introducing the notion of "pre-religion," to do justice to the worlds of people among whom one cannot find the forms of religious organizations that historians describe. (This notion also marks his break from the Durkheimian search for elementary forms of religious life). This should be pondered by anybody interested in the hypothesis of our century exhibiting diverse forms of "post-religion."

Claude Lévi-Strauss (born 1908)

Upon his arrival in Brazil Claude Lévi-Strauss resolved to travel West to the Mato Grosso and do fieldwork among the native Indian populations. His interest for ethnography was aroused by reading the book by Robert Lowie, *Primitive Society* (1920). He has to his credit numerous scientific publications but also the writing of a narrative, *Tristes Tropiques* (1955). The account of his travel is mixed with presentation (in layman's terms) of his findings and abundant reflexive pages. These pages refer also to his other travels in Asia and North America. They tell a story of disenchantment. At the end of his (difficult) Brazilian travel, his group finally came in contact with "uncontaminated" natives. But, running short of supplies and many being sick, the group was then rushing back to "civilization" and could only ascertain that these Indians had indeed never met any members of "Western civilization" and spoke an unknown language. Lévi-Strauss then discusses the classical pages of Rousseau on "natural man" and agrees that no new magical key is to be found by going to the ends of the inhabited world.

Lévi-Strauss managed to do away with the talk of "primitive people". He preferred the designation of *peuples sans écriture* ("people without writing"). His structuralist method of studying the myths of American Indians described their organization and reconstructed the underlying world of thought conditioning all cultural creations. Bastide contrasts Lévi-Strauss intellectualist distanciation from what the indigenous people narrate with his own interest in the affective dimension present in the discourse that meets the experience of time by telling some sort of story. His interest is not just for the structures of the mind, but also for the way the whole human being lives. Lévi-Strauss admitted having no interest in the practices of sacrifice because they are not part of thinking, but part of praxis, namely of a world of confusion and participation. With Lévy-Brühl (and Leenhardt), Bastide is interested in confusion.

Lévi-Strauss also gave currency to the distinction between cold and hot societies. Cold societies, those studied by ethnologists, produce very little disorder. They tend to maintain themselves in their original state, which led Europeans to say that they had no history and ignored progress, both unwarranted generalizations. Hot societies like ours discuss their structures, admit internal conflicts, and practise self-government by majority rule. Thus 50% plus one can destroy the old unanimous consent and bring about a new consensus. Lévi-Strauss adds that *cold* and *hot* are ideal types and that no society is ever a pure embodiment of the model.

The historian Fernand Braudel (one of the young Frenchmen in São Paulo in the late 1930s) invited his fellow historians to study not just events but also trends in the *longue durée*, namely enduring patterns that maintain themselves through the centuries. There are "cold" layers even in an apparently volatile modern nation like France.

Chapter 4

"Civilizations neither meet nor clash; people do"[1]

Founded in 1934, the University of São Paulo was energized in the social sciences by the arrival of a group of gifted young French scholars, nearly all of whom were to achieve world-wide reputation. Among them was historian Fernand Braudel, geographer Pierre Monbeig and "sociologist" Claude Lévi-Strauss. Lévi-Strauss taught for only one year and does not seem to have left positive memories in academic circles. Bastide was selected to succeed him and in June 1938 arrived with his family in São Paulo. They were to stay until 1954 (Bastide returned afterward for shorter stays.)

World War II probably influenced Bastide's decision to remain in Brazil. Like De Gaulle, Bastide was aware of the visibility of Nazis in Argentina and of the authority of Vichy in the French Embassies in the Americas, so he wrote to defend the cause of the Free French. But sheer intellectual excitement in the discovery of the new country must have also loomed large in the mind of the expatriate. He taught and wrote in French, but he quickly understood Portuguese. His attempts to speak it were said to reflect rather a variety of Languedocien.

Bastide promptly read everything that was written on the sociology of Brazil. By 1939 articles and book reviews begin to pour forth from his pen. But his social immersion was mainly among artists, and his first lectures were on the aesthetics and the philosophy and sociology of art. Since 1922 São Paulo had been the locus of all sorts of revivals in literature and in the visual arts, shaking off the yoke of colonial reliance upon models drawn from the prestigious traditions of Europe, mainly of France. So the intellectuals he frequented were art critics, poets, writers, painters and architects. He followed the new developments in film and theater. All these avant-garde circles were clearly left-leaning. None of them catered to the tastes of the rich and francophile Brazilian bourgeoisie. A Black empowerment movement, *Frente Negra Brasileira* had started in São Paulo in 1931. Bastide also noticed the rise of a Black Press and followed the activities

Short history of Brazil

In 1500 a Portuguese sailor, Pedro Alvares Cabral, landed upon a beach in the South Atlantic, from which he saw a very dense forest. In 1494 the Pope had drawn a line meant to prevent competition for empire between Spain and Portugal. To the West of it, the Gulf of Mexico explored by Spain, to the East the coasts of Africa where Portugal had been active for some time. The beach in South America is for Portugal. After exporting wood, the Portuguese started developing sugar plantations and brought African slaves as work force. Thus began a cycle of agricultural booms; after sugar and cocoa came coffee and soy. Gold, gems and diamonds were found in the eighteenth century.

Brazil's path to independence was unlike any other in the Americas. In 1807 Napoleon invaded Portugal and the king, his court and the government moved to Rio de Janeiro. They returned in 1821 and left the king's son as viceroy. The local elites, who had gained a taste for self-government, proclaimed independence in 1822. They also offered a constitutional imperial crown to the viceroy. His son Pedro II came to the throne in 1831 and inaugurated a long and fondly remembered reign, as his personal skills established a balance between liberal progressive ideas and conservative interests. The quality of administration improved, European immigration was welcomed, growth was exceptional, and industrial development began. The emancipation of slaves was done progressively and completed without a civil war, and in 1888 all are made free. In 1889 the monarchy was abolished and the Republic proclaimed. However there were storms in the history of the Republic, the worst being the military regime of 1964–1985. In 1989 direct presidential election was restored.

Until the availability of air transportation, only the coastal cities were in frequent and easy (but slow) contact. People who had the means to travel tended to go to Europe (especially France) rather than elsewhere in their country. The transfer of the capital from Rio de Janeiro to Brasilia (founded in 1955 deep in the interior) moved the centre of gravity of the country and helped develop the potential of the West. Brazil now has about 200 millions inhabitants, is the fifth largest country in the world, has more land suitable for agriculture that any other country.

of the *Teatro Experimental do Negro* in the 1940s. He observed that the African theatre was emancipating itself from the stereotypes that confined it to vulgar comedies for white audiences and how it became more dramatic—and more relevant to the condition of Afro-Brazilians audiences.[2] While Lévi-Strauss headed West from São Paulo to meet Indians in the forest, Bastide remained in the city and made himself into what one would call now an urban anthropologist. Starting in 1938 Bastide went through a voluntary process of acculturation. He began to live in two languages.

The artistic creative ebullience of São Paulo occurred in what was the most industrialized, most prosperous and most educated part of the country. But another literary revolution was also occurring in the Nordeste, the heartland of the old colonial sugar plantations and of what remained of the old African slave culture. The society that had developed around the land monopoly maintained by the descendants of the colonial owners of large estates (latifundia) had the highest level of malnutrition and the lowest level of literacy in the area with the richest land of Brazil.[3] In the 1920s the fame of itinerant illiterate rural poets spread in this famished world and their work became known outside the villages. They worked within the genre of the A.B.C. poems: series of narrative quatrains starting with the succession of letters in the alphabet. Some tell love stories, others tales of the rise and fall of messianic leaders. Stories also abound about the feats of local heroes, "bandits of honour," bandits with style and a social cause since, eloquent in their acts, they avenge impoverished and oppressed people. Small local presses started printing inexpensive leaflets with these tales. Sold by itinerant peddlers, they were highly successful. These popular hagiographies draw happily from the records of Christian saints, the stories of African gods and bits of Indian tales. Poetry achieves a perfect syncretistic blend.

A young generation of novelists was born in this literary milieu and achieved stature, the greatest of them being Jorge Amado who became a member of the Communist Party.[4] Through them Brazilian literature began to deal with little people, traditionally voiceless, and sounded the voice of social protest. Toward the end of his life, Bastide wrote a study on Jorge Amado that showed how this author transformed the poetic and naturalist genres by drawing from the art of Afro-Brazilian tellers of tales. He also showed how Amado managed to be religious (in a syncretistic vein) and political at the same time.[5]

Giving an account of Bastide's first years in his new country, Maria Isaura Pereira de Queiroz writes that this Frenchman considered that appreciation of the current innovative artistic creation in Brazil was the essential part of his initiation into the country and its culture. Moreover Bastide was not busy working on yet another sociology of art but was rather inventing a new sociological aesthetics.[6] Two books came out in Portuguese: *A Poesia Afro-Brasileira* (1943)[7] in which he began to wrestle with the problem of inter-penetration of cultures, and *Arte e sociedade* (1945, 2nd ed. 1971). The second book, drawn from his university lectures, was translated into French in 1977.[8] It refers to previous French authors and uses such key notions as the difference between aesthetic and anaes-

Jorge Amado (1912–2001)

The great Brazilian novelist of the twentieth century who collected numerous international literary prizes and was translated into 31 languages, was born on a cocoa plantation in the Northeast, son of the owner. He ran away from the residential Jesuit college in Salvador de Bahia to which his family had sent him. He accepted to resume his studies in a more liberal-minded environment. He led an urban bohemian life, and read eagerly avant-garde authors. He published his first novel *Cacau* (Cocoa) at 19 and joined socialist militant groups. His early works take for granted cordiality between the descendants of the Indians, the Africans and the Portuguese (the group to which his family belongs) and solidarity among the victims of injustice. His fictions breathe social militancy; they sell but shock the literary establishment. Bastide locates him in the school of naturalism but finds a contrast with the works of Zola. With Amado the material crudity is there but so is the proximity to tropical nature, the sea and night skies; his literature of the proletariat remains penetrated with folklore and celebration of life, such as it is. Bastide finds there a perfect blend between document and poetry. Obviously the narrative skills of this Brazilian were learned in the streets of Bahia from Afro-Brazilians, from men and women, old and young, and were not spoiled by a classical education. He labels his art *réalisme merveilleux* (realism with wonders). Bastide met him in Bahia in 1945 and was introduced by him to life in the Northeast.

In 1935 and 1936 Amado was arrested on grounds of being a member of the Communist Party. There began for him then periods of exile. Amado left the party in 1956 and returned to Brazil for good—and for a career of prolific writing. His later works are great, long, wild tales, with a new dimension of humour in the manner of Rabelais. Many of them were made into Brazilian TV series, and the translations were well received in the US. These later works remain true to two aspects of his early novels: the legendary brigands that people remember are identified with Saint George who slays the dragon, and the religion of Candomblé is ever-present. Syncretism of Christianity, Indian and African religions is not talked about but poetically practised.

thetic facts. It quotes Zola's taunt to the French republicans: you want to get rid of the King, of God and of the social order, but leave untouched the old literature and academic art. With his usual capacity for a cautious degree of systematization, Bastide argues that art can be:

1. An expression of society.
2. A technique for forgetting it.
3. A reaction against it (often).
4. A play in the margins of it (nearly always).

Sociologies of art institutions already existed; in these pages Bastide opens the way for a broader, more ambitious undertaking, namely the sociology of art itself. In a similar manner, sociology of religion will embrace more topics than the sociology or religious institutions, which frequently remain at the level of sociographies.[9]

Bastide also stresses that aesthetic and religious activities appear simultaneously in the early days of humankind. He concludes that words and works of art are episodes in processes of symbolic exchange and should not be considered as things. Society is an effect of art just as art is a product of society. (The halo of art may start to be compared with that of magic). Works of art must be included among the data that enable sociologists to get hold of the social. They put them on the track of the metamorphoses of collective sensibilities. Works of art draw attention to dreams of historical imaginary, and of the variations in the systems of classification and the visions of the world reigning in the various groups that make the society as a whole and its uneasy hierarchies. The basic theoretical sources of *Arte e Sociedade* come from the France of the late nineteenth and twentieth centuries, but the lines of argument reflect an immersion in the Brazilian realities the author had under his eyes.

In his 1977 preface to *Art et société* Jean Duvignaud argues that Bastide discovered in Brazil the dynamism and force of the imaginary. There he saw that art and symbols are the best resource humans have to go round the obstacles that hinder the communication of consciences. Art is necessary to overcome isolation. Duvignaud quotes a page from Bastide's book on Gide:

> individual selves need some secrecy to protect themselves from the hold others gain over them; they however also invent artistic forms to express themselves. They seek thereby to achieve not instant communication, but a differed one that opens the possibility of relations that do not yet exist.[10]

Thus the literature Bastide read in his youth and the Parisian circles he frequented in his early adulthood provided him with the base for a deeper understanding of what the life of culture was all about. His experience of the São Paulo avant-garde artistic circles expanded on that. In the end, his reflections on art and literature led to improved conceptualizations of acculturation and hybridation. It nourished his sustained explorations into the social phenomena of race relations and inter-penetration of cultures.[11] A whole new chapter of sociology was about to be born.

Maria Isaura Pereira de Queiroz informs us that Bastide quickly saw the need to revise his European categories in the light of the new social realities he was becoming cognizant of. Having read all the published work of previous Brazilian social scientists, he judged that they had been too quick in assimilating French categories, their clear thinking and sharp contrasts. European ethnocentrism had been uncritically assimilated in social scientific circles. Specifically the contrasts between black skin and white skin had been made into a hard opposition when in fact the lines in Brazil had been blurred for quite some time. So Bastide helped bring to the social science tradition the same sort of cultural revolution that the artists of São Paulo (and of the Northeast) had brought in their opposition in the 1920s to academic criteria of art.[12] Science had to be nationalized to become attentive to national realities.[13]

A comparison has been drawn between Bastide and Pierre Monbeig, the French geographer who went to Brazil at the same time. These scholars of the *Mission française* were supposed to export the excellence of French universities. In fact, none of them had had university positions; they were all young men in search of adventure. When Monbeig undertook to research the history of land occupation in the Province of São Paulo, he found that what he had learned in France was of little help. The sources were of a different kind; he had to cope with phenomena of considerable internal migration and with new patterns of urbanization. Enjoying the lack of institutional constraints, Monbeig broke free from acquired conceptualizations and ended up removing the great Vidal de la Blache, founder of modern French geography, from his pedestal. This parallels what Bastide did to Durkheim, the *patron* of French sociologists in the first decades of the twentieth century.[14]

M.I. Pereira de Queiroz shows in an important article that what Bastide learned from Mauss and Gurvitch led him both to penetrating views of the variety of cultural trends and religious phenomena in Brazilian society, and to healthy doubts about the degree of integration achieved. To talk of homogeneity, equilibrium and harmony, Bastide repeatedly argues, is not appropriate for sociologists. Such terms are parts of value judgments. In his view, ethnic and cultural differences, differences in education, economic differences, differences in social class, are in constant movement; all sides meet in unceasing differentiation, leading thus to new contrasts, new conflicts, and new complementarities.[15]

Note that Bastide, from then on, adheres to an apparent rule of two-way traffic in cultural communication. Claude Ravelet counted his output during the years 1939–1945. It totalled four books, 217 articles and 81 book reviews: 47 articles are on De Gaulle, the French anti-nazi Resistance and its writers; 32 on French literature (classical and contemporary); 67 on Brazilian literature; 28 on the sociology of Brazil; and 18 on Brazilian sociology. As a rule what is meant for France is published in the original and what is for Brazil is translated.[16]

Thus Bastide made an important contribution to the great ongoing national debate about the Brazilian identity. Reflexive Brazilians and other intelligent observers are perplexed as they note the enormous contrast between the wealth and culture of some and the poverty of many. There is also a contrast between the relaxed nature of inter-racial relations and the persistent inequalities, between manifest ease and agreeableness of mores and fits of social and political violence. The familiar lines of the debates are dualistic. M.I. Pereira de Queiroz points out that as early as the nineteenth century the great duality was thought of in terms of skin colour and often carried pessimistic accounts about the possibility of raising the slaves to a desirable level of civilization. This led to a short-lived policy of favouring European immigration. (It also led to the creation in Pernambuco, for instance, an official government "Service for the Protection of Psychopaths," which sought to defend the adherents of Black cults while controlling their institutions[17]). Note that in the twentieth century the emancipated descendants of the slaves either stayed in the Northeast or moved to rest of the country in search of jobs. Marxist class analyses focused on the urban proletariat that was concentrated in the industrialized Province of São Paulo in the twentieth century and did not fail to see the importance of the colour bar. The result was that the sweeping phenomena of cultural syncretism tended to become obscured.

The simple views of the contrast between Black and White were challenged with the publication of an epoch-making book, *Casa Grande e Senzala* (1933) by Gilberto Freyre. The author was trained in the US school of anthropology and the book rapidly received a wide diffusion.[18] The culture of Brazil is unified, argues Freyre, but it is based on the sort of duality that existed inside the big Portuguese sugar plantations between the masters and the African slaves that were brought to work for them. His book contrasts the manor of the land-owning family with the dwelling quarters of the slaves. Brazilians organized in their plantations a patriarchal system on a grandiose scale. Unlike other European slaveholders in America, those in Brazil took pride in the number of slave women they got pregnant and included the offspring they had from them in their visible, apparently happy retinue. They also ordinarily emancipated them in their will. The godfather and godmother system required by the Catholic Church also played a role. Leading Portuguese families accompanied some slave infants to the baptismal fonts and pronounced their vows for them. Godchildren received support for education, and sometimes got money for emancipation. In the plantations, their parents and family get a measure of protection, and the family of the masters receives assurance of loyal domestic serv-

The Freyre Thesis

Any discussion of the moral ills caused by colonialism must be aware of the different policies pursued by the colonial powers. Scholars should know the historical facts before discussing patterns of exploitation and their complex moral dimensions. Gilberto Freyre (1966) has advanced a thesis on the singularity of the practises espoused by the Portuguese colonists.

As Portuguese sailors, merchants, adventurers and colonists explored the West Coast of Africa (they rounded the tip of South Africa in 1488), they decided to develop settlements and judged that the only way to populate the area they seized was by having children with the indigenous women, having them baptized and raising them in Portuguese. They knew that Portugal was a small country without much population to spare and their social class did not share the obsession for "purity of blood" that characterized most of their Spanish neighbours. This policy, which greatly helped the settlers adapt to their new life conditions, had been practised for about a century before the Portuguese undertook to colonize their lands in what is now Brazil. While the system obviously met the sexual needs of the enterprising adventurers, it also indicates their fondness for (male dominated) family.

It did not take long for power in Brazil to be in the hands of the patriarchs of the leading extended families with their vast estates. The children were first obtained from Indian women—who had "higher standards of cleanliness"—but quickly changed mainly to children from African slaves. History books either celebrate or just indicate the case of Jeronimo de Albuquerque (d. 1584) who recognized twenty-four mixed race children, and made sure they all found a place in the elite of the new country. (The status of the child always depended on that of the father). Neither the Church in Rome nor the Crown in Lisbon could undermine this emerging power structure, and there is no evidence that they tried very hard to curb this kind of population increase. Thus, states Freyre, the cultural foundation of Brazilian society is a mixture of aristocracy, democracy and anarchy.

ices.[19] This social system creates what has been labelled the *cordial man* (*homem cordial*), prompt at establishing affective bonds and at welcoming newcomers in the existing extended family, on the tacit condition that no change is made to the power structure. This cultural pattern blurs the distinction between private and public life; seeing others as potential family members prevents seeing them as citizens.[20] In the extended patriarchal family, sex is not secret or shameful, but desirable because fecund. The same attitude prevails in the Church, except among Jesuits. Priests and friars were especially successful in providing good education and brilliant futures to their offspring.

Freyre's book nourished the legends of the erotic splendour and abundance of luso-tropicalism.[21] Interracial relations are then seen only through the rhythm of the samba and the photographs of *futebol* stars; the whole is painted with the colours of dances, music, physical beauty and athletic achievement. Mieko Nishida quotes a succinct expression of the contrast between Brazil and the US on matters of race and colour: "in Brazil the mulatto has been seen as evidence that the population was becoming white, whereas in the United States as becoming black."[22] Such comparisons however should not hide past and present realities of sexual oppression and economic domination. Commenting on the numerous texts of colonial era clerics blaming the sensuous African women for debauching Portuguese Catholic men, Freyre insists that African genes do not explain anything, but slavery explains a lot. The young African women were not seduced but ordered about. White boys felt free to molest Black playmates and got the habit of command.[23] Since all the land was for sugar, slaves could not get a plot of land for subsistence farming; they had to live (if that is the word) on manioc-based meals. The infant mortality rate was high and the Northeast had some of the world's worst forms of malnutrition and poverty until late in the twentieth century. This being said, it remains an important fact that, under Portuguese law, slaves who saved enough money were able to purchase their freedom.[24] Another law granted automatic emancipation to women who had given birth ten (later seven) times. And the first step toward massive emancipation was the Law of the Free Womb: after 1871 no one is born a slave.

Baudrillard's contrast between real and symbolic power may help analyse the complex interactions in these patriarchal households. The Portuguese hold power, and their rule is firmly established. But the young women slaves have bodies that make the white men dream. Should they not try to use sex to their advantage? "Seduction represents mastery of the symbolic universe, while all that power represents is mastery of the real world."[25] Isn't their participation in the symbolic world the chink in the armour the powerful wear?

In his article on racism in Brazil, Bastide makes a decisive factual observation: the proportion of the population that occupied the spectrum of colour somewhere between the extremes of pure white and pure black kept growing rapidly in the nineteenth century. And this undoubtedly facilitated the path to universal legal emancipation. At the time of the Emancipation in 1888, a very large group in the country paid little or no attention to shades of colour.[26] Freyre was himself issued from one of the great land-owning families that had fallen into bad twentieth century days. There is clearly some nostalgia in his account of the old mores. He wrote a chapter entitled “The Negro slave in the sexual and family life of the Brazilian” and used the first person plural. “We almost all ‘bear the mark’ of the Negro wet nurse, of the mulatto girl who showed us how to get rid of the *bicho de pe*” (a parasite that burrows below the skin of the foot), and of the one who later “gave us our first complex sensation of being a man.”[27] His “optimistic” view of a significant interaction and even of cultural homogeneity arising from sexual promiscuity (which before his book had been mentioned only to be deplored) is grounded in real facts and thus could take some hold.[28] It does shed light on the ongoing proclivity of Brazilians to produce offspring and even marry outside the colour or ethnic bars that prevent this behaviour in many other countries. “Miscegenation” (to use the term familiar to students of US history and law) occurred on three fronts: Portuguese with Indians and Africans, Indians with Africans and Portuguese, and, of course, Africans with Indians and Portuguese. In time, it was simpler to label everyone Brazilian.[29] (Christian and family names have also become so mixed up that they are no indication of ethnicity, religion or skin colour).

It is not surprising therefore that Bastide’s work was well received in his new country. He got abundant recognition in Brazil, most significantly with the Order of the Cruzeiro do Sul (1954). Three of his numerous students achieved exceptional national prominence in the sociology of religion: Florestan Fernandes studied the social prospects of Afro-Brazilians in the new industrialized economics. (He was also elected to Congress). Maria Isaura Pereira de Queiroz studied the messianic movements and placed them in the worldwide context of such intensely religious moments. And Fernando Henrique Cardoso, anthropologist, became president of the Republic.[30]

Chapter 5

The three books on Afro-Brazilian religions

What was to be Bastide's magnum opus are accounts of the process of cultural reproduction among a group exposed to forced acculturation, the Afro-Brazilians, first brought as slaves to the colonial Northeast dominated by the sugar economy, and later participating in forms of mutual cultural inter-penetration in a pluralist society. This work led to three books that made Candomblé known to the world and that still make Bastide an important source for any work on theories of religions. His studies focused first on the African cults present in Bahia[1] where many people kept dark skin colour, next in other locations of Northeast Brazil, and finally in the South, where the pigmentation generally got lighter.

Here too it matters to know the genesis of the scholarly endeavour. In the summer of 1943–1944, more precisely in January–February of 1944, Bastide did a study tour (or fieldwork session) in the area of Bahia and Recife. He had read up all that the Brazilian authors had written on the cults that the Bahian population (slaves and their descendants) had developed. He also came with a series of excellent contacts. But, once on the site, he cut some moorings, from books and from his academic environment, because experience conveyed to him some fresh meanings that were self-evident. Now he meets people, he sees and hears much, including *carnaval*. He is made aware of the vitality of the descendants of the slaves brought to Brazil, victims of one of the major instances of inhumanity, namely the transportation and exploitation of African slaves, as America was colonized by Europeans. We observe here one of these cases in intellectual biographies when it is not the scholar who chooses his topic, but the topic that chooses the scholar. The trip therefore has an initiatory quality.

This is reflected in a text he published shortly afterward in Portuguese entitled *Imagens de Nordeste mistico em branco et preto* (1945). Recent efforts to find the French original have been in vain. So the French-speaking public has a re-translation.[2]

The book admits at the outset that it does not fit within a clear genre, hovering as it does between poetic narrative and scientific essay. Describing the sea, the beach and the fishing boats, the opening page tells that the people in Salvador de Bahia name their boats after women or after saints, "since they don't know any more whether they love the saints with a carnal love, or their wives with a spiritual one." The whole text is flushed with tropical colour and suggestions of sensuality. The reader is exposed to bumps in the texts, openings or faults that are usually censored in conventional "scientific prose."[3] A "sheaf of images," it is yet more than a literary travel narrative because of the amount of historical and anthropological information.[4] Maristela Oliveira de Andrade has contrasted Bastide's travel narrative, written practically on the spot, with that of Lévi-Strauss composed nearly twenty years after his exposure to the new world. Is Bastide baroque and romantic? Or is he just enchanted seeing baroque art and romantic scenes? In any case Bastide's pen conveys the strength of the new visual impacts to which the author was exposed. The text abounds in images.[5]

The first chapter deals with churches and Catholic festivals. Near the shore is a great marble baroque church, brought stone by stone from Portugal. Another one, possibly bigger, was likewise transported from the Mother Country; the ship bringing it however sank in the bay so it still lies there unassembled. And there is the one built from local material, on the directions of a native woman who was informed in a dream that the Virgin Mary had crossed the ocean. A statue of her embracing the child was indeed found on the shore. To get acclimatized, Christianity had to be brought by hands other than Portuguese ones. The description of the great church and cloister of San Francesco draws the attention to three features. First Bastide stresses the sober straight lines of the Portuguese baroque; soft colours, good proportions, elegant turrets; no curved walls in the Roman and Spanish manner. After the quiet and luminous elegance comes an exuberant inside, an abundance of swirling sculptures and straining caryatids, vibrating stucco, dark woods, and plenty of gold leaf. The technique of ecstasy in this church, he adds, is similar to that of the Afro-Brazilian, but moves the eyes through intense and dramatic sculpture rather than through bodies dancing to the sound of the drums. Then there is the contrast between the spiritual excess of the sanctuary designed to wrench humans from this world, and the quiet repose of the scenes painted on blue tiles (*asulejos)* in the cloister, with their citations from Horace on worldly wisdom and on following nature. Finally Bastide draws the contrast with the Mexican baroque, which is much more tormented, with deep relief in the façades creating shade in the midst of light, and an abundance of tortured scenes and skulls, as if Aztec scenes of gore had stirred the imagination of the Spanish monks. To be sure, there are wounded saints and Christs in Bahia, but nothing of the morbidity found in the Spanish North. Piety here is much less ferocious (more Thomistic, says the theologically informed visitor).

The discussion of Afro-Brazilian cults begins with a bluntly expressed opposition to the apparently received view: these cults are not the rigid and barbarian practices of non-civilized people arrested in their development, but a subtle thought that has not yet been deciphered. (Is Bastide thinking of Champollion's work with the hieroglyphs?) This religion is not one of ascent of the soul to God but of descent of the gods upon their sons and daughters, who, in trances, are ridden as if they were horses. Africanists had identified the pattern on their continent—and noted that the processes intensify when Africans come in contact with Europeans. On both sides of the Atlantic, numerous rites (initiation, for instance) are based on the premise that people get born and die in stages.

The cults in Bahia exemplify a successful attempt to reproduce a culture under adverse circumstances. Transportation across the Atlantic detribalized the African slaves and mutilated the memories of those who survived the crossing of the ocean. In the Bahian cults some form of tribal belonging is reconstituted, each tribe having a distinctive site (the *terreiro*, where the temple complex is built), where distinctive gods (*orixa*) are honoured. After a review of the personnel of the cult, comes the description of Candomblé, the public, festive celebration. A lively description is given of the joyful business in the preparation. Bastide writes of happy pride in continuation of heritage; he sees the celebrations as adding *douceur* to Brazilian life conditions. The ritual has four stages. In the morning an animal is sacrificed that will provide the meat. In the evening, when all are assembled, drums call the gods and a circular dance begins; the gods descend on some people—mainly women. Then some of the initiates dance dressed as the gods. Finally a festive meal is served to all on banana leaves. On the trances, Bastide immediately rallies to the view of Herskovits, the US anthropologist who had recently observed them in Bahia: the phenomenon is not pathological but a normal part of a cultural whole; it follows in an orderly manner some collective representations. Human bodies are cultured bodies; trances are not an exit from culture. In these powerfully physical events, the social is prior to the mystical.[6] The desire for the trance is a desire for a metamorphosis, and reflects a need to compensate for daily experience.

Bastide then, and quite consistently, argues against any separation of the rites from the myths. So he gives a portrait of three of the *orixa: Exu, Oxala* and *Yemanja,* with reference to the legends about African kings whose actions they imitate; he gives the text of the hymns sung at their festivals. In some syncretistic versions, *Exu* has been assimilated to the devil—which is quite misleading since all the gods have ambivalent sides, *Exu* only more.[7] *Oxala* is an old man, the father of all the gods; "his" church is washed annually in a great three-day festival. He is said to own a church, which on city maps is labeled *Our Lord of Bomfin*, a baroque masterpiece on a hill just outside of Bahia. In time (and with help from the police) the clergy managed to obtain that the "folkloric" custom washes only the front steps. *Yemanja* is the beautiful goddess of the sea, a siren known for her vanity, with mirror, comb, golden hair and a tail of shiny scales. Her feast culminates in great offerings thrown into the bay. She is said to make sailors happy to drown.

The chapters on Recife describe a different baroque style, more rococo and curvy. Bastide saw in one a Black African Saint Michael victorious over an evil Roman legionnaire who is of course as white and pink as can be. The pages also show the difference between the *xango* celebrated there and Bahia's *Candomblé.* The Afro-Brazilian population in Recife is more proletarianized and the colour bar more visible. Bastide raises the question of degeneration in this cult. Blood sacrifices are more frequent and so is police persecution. The dances he saw were of the carnival type and featured coronation of kings of the Congo and of Mozambique. Distinctive also is the feast of the *ignama*.

Much more visible around Recife is the presence of the Indian. Escaping or emancipated slaves ran into the hinterland. In some cases, they founded their own villages, but mostly mixed with the Indians. The *sertao* there is a quite distinct geographical area. The land is poor, the rain infrequent. It sustains an economy based on the raising of cattle and horses.[8] Periodic droughts cause famine and dispersal of population. This is the land of the *cabocles*, a term which attests to the indifference about racial descent since it can mean the "civilized" Indian (i.e. who speaks some Portuguese and entered the national economy), the mixed race Indian (the other half being black or white), or just the poor peasant. Unlike the African gods who can descend anywhere, the spirits of the *cabocles* are always localized. The cult relies on tobacco and on a drink from the *jurema* tree. Available mythology is scant. The ceremonies are often consultation for treatment of some ill. They are not very festive. The participants sit a lot in front of a very composite altar. Bastide proposes to place the rituals more on the magic end of the spectrum between religion and magic. He also suggests that the Africans of the *sertao* took to the way of the *cabocles* in order to acknowledge the land they were now living in.

The conclusion meditates on the crucial notions of bodily-enacted rhythm and of rhythm shared. Streets are very narrow and steep in Bahia so strong Black workingmen keep carrying things in groups, loading and unloading them in rhythm with work songs. Likewise with the fishermen, hauling their boats or their nets. The *capoeira* is a vigorous and acrobatic dance for young men, aping deadly fight, but in which the "combatants" do not touch.[9] The marches and the processions, the music and the songs, the dances and drums in Candomblé, are all part of the same union of kinaesthetic, aesthetics and religion, fostering the communion of Brazilian hearts.[10]

In 1958, another book was published focussing on *Candomblé* in Bahia.[11] The author had in the meantime contributed a few specialized articles and this time dips his pen in different ink. The vein is less lyrical and not so participatory. Conventionally, the book begins with a review of the existing literature. Scholarship is a cumulative affair. Predecessors forged a language and fresh research may keep it in use, qualify it, or reject it. As early as 1896, the Bahian rites were described carefully by Nina Rodrigues, a young doctor in Salvador. Rodrigues belongs to the great generation of positivists; he recruited his informers carefully and worked very conscientiously. His *métier* consisted in describing what he observed, with great minutia. He was also a forensic doctor and psychiatrist (schooled in the views of Dr. Pierre Janet)—and a racist who considered the inferiority of the Blacks as scientifically established. Such categories as hysteria, animism and fetishism are for him firmly established scientific concepts. Father Etienne Ignace Brazil also published on Afro-Brazilian cults but relied exclusively on the work of Rodrigues, only adding to them the notion of idolatry and his theological disapproval. A man with darker skin, Manuel Querino, finally did write (1916, 1922) on the Africans in Bahia. He is not a trained ethnographer but adds the voice of one concerned to establish a positive contribution of the people of Candomblé to the overall Brazilian civilization. Scientific progress is brought about by Arthur Ramos who is alert to the needs of objectivity, and has increased awareness of the work done in Africa and of the general trend in North American cultural anthropology. Melville J. Herskovits came to Bahia in 1942, in the context of his research on the Africans in the New World. His contribution was decisive since it placed the cults in the overall context of the social life. Herskovits was determined to show that the slaves who set foot on the Americas were not savage animals devoid of any semblance of human culture. He proved his point and opened a new field of research: the slaves came with their past.[12] His work is now considered tainted by the frequent recourse to the idea of simple survival of African forms.[13]

The 1958 book shows that, since his 1944 sojourn in the Northeast, Bastide had acquainted himself with the work of Marcel Griaule

(1898–1956) on the Dogon of Africa.[14] This strengthened his resolve to interpret the data without recourse to the categories of Western mentality. He salutes therefore the contribution of Lévy-Brühl, who alerted ethnologists to the need to develop appropriate vocabularies to do justice to the difference in mentalities. The book begins with a full description of Candomblé rites and their location. The evening ceremony begins with offerings to *Exu* and a polite request asking him to leave and not disturb the proceedings. The entry of the participants is slow—and so is the exit. The hierarchy is complex. In the Bantu cults, the *babalorixa* (usually a man) is the head of the ceremony. With the Yoruba, the presidency belongs to a woman, the *ialorixa*. These presiding leaders are selected from the sons or daughters of the gods, namely the initiates. The chapter on sacred space and time is a meticulous attempt to give an account of the mentality by understanding the myths. Each Candomblé is a summary of the whole of Africa. There is a central pillar around which the daughters dance. The bowls, the drums and other musical instruments are all parts of a cosmological whole. The ceremonies repair or strengthen the world. Each *terreiro* (temple complex) has its own sacred calendar. No ceremonies take place during Catholic Holy Week, one of many overlaps between the two cults. Links are seen between *Oxala* and Christ. *Oxala* is associated with Friday, which becomes the day of the celebration of Heaven. The calendar adapted to the seven-day week, which replaced the African one of four or five days. Social communion rests on a diversity of liturgical functions. Material and spiritual organization go together.

The personnel or priesthood of Candomblé is varied. The *babalao* had highest rank in Africa but have no visible role in the great public ceremonies of Bahia. They are the experts in the consultation of the goddess *Ifa*. Their role is thus divinatory. Their role extends beyond the *terreiro* since they learn from *Ifa* to which god a prospective initiate belongs. Supporting him the *babalosaim* goes in the forest to gather the herbs necessary for washing the head of the prospective initiate, and the *babaoge* obtains the required permission from the ancestors (the *egun*). No god ever rides these "officials." The procedures of divination show a four-fold division of the cosmos, with the *orixa* clearly beyond, since they are the principles of classification of the events in it. To be thinkable, the cosmos must be cut up in parts. In Africa the *orixa* were gods of specific clans. In Brazil the clans have disappeared and the classification has become purely religious, expressing the logic of relations between diversified realities.

Exu is a god unlike the others. Africanists have classified him as trickster; his features as an unpredictable little demon have led to a rapprochement with the Christians' devil. Some informers identify him as protector of the Blacks; others, who condone the use of black magic, make of him the *orixa* who helps the hurting or the killing (but does not hurt or kill) the Whites. In Candomblé that stays clear of any magic, he remains the bad boy who is a useful intermediary between humans and the gods (and thus sometimes identified with saint Anthony or Saint Peter). Bastide sees him as the god of openings, of doors and paths, namely as the dialectic element in the cosmos that punches holes in the walls separating the four parts of the cosmos, and thus, somewhat paradoxically, the god of order. (Does it take disorder for human living to be ordered?)

Turning to the ritual, Bastide elaborates the now familiar argument about ecstasies always following cultural models. We might say trances are halfway between theatre as we know it and the crises of severely affected people in mental hospitals before the advent of tranquillizing drugs. Ecstasies repeat an archaic past, he now proposes. They share the same structure as the myth. The traditional gestures are acted out and become a lived reality. Possession by the god is transformation of the personality. The individual is both the author and not the author of his/her own action. The face and the body are metamorphosed. Trances are not purely individual; they also take place within a context of interference, response and support from other dancers. They therefore include a dialogue among the initiates possessed by the gods. So the dance is carefully regulated; some dancers in a normal state of consciousness follow attentively those who are ridden by the gods. After the exit from the trance, the individuals who have been seized are kindly led to recovery rooms.[15]

At this point Bastide believes he has gathered enough data for describing an "African anthropology." Society is formed by the communion between humans and gods. Candomblé are spiritual families replacing the lost clans. (One cannot marry someone who has the same *orixa*). Humans are reflections of the gods. The creation of the world comes from the union of heaven and earth; humans are likewise born of sexual union. Union with the *orixa* is source of strengths of all kinds. The higher the rank in the hierarchy, the stricter the limitations on behaviour. High-ranking people receive respect and have obligations to the community. Far from being an orgy, the cult is an ethic, of solidarity through mutual giving. The initiates are individuals on their own, with a soul and a guardian angel. The individual is always at the crossroads between personal destiny and relationship with the god. The sacred is thus both transcendent and immanent.

The conclusion stresses that African mythologies have been re-thought in the context of the New World. The sociologist should attempt archaeological work. Historical events and contingencies added new elements and transformed the older framework. Bastide ventures a generalization: history in such series of events stretches timeless metaphysics to breaking points.

As is the case with Africans, participation is a common category of thought in Bahia; the same African god can be at the same time a god and a Catholic saint. So Lévy-Brühl is right in his analysis of "primitive mentality". But this is not to say that these Africans and their Brazilian descendants are incapable of acknowledging objective contradiction when they see it. They demonstrate ability to use both connecting and separating types of thinking. Bahians are quite aware of a gap between the cult and daily Brazilian life. This Bastide calls *principe de coupure*.[16] People can live without drama in two different worlds. This principle opens the way to diversity among what we call logical modes of thinking. Drawing upon the work of Piaget on the mental operations of children, Bastide suggests that within the world of Candomblé the logic of complementarity keeps resisting the logic of boxes within boxes that Western taxonomies have favoured since Aristotle.

The final observations give a few principles relevant to the sociology of knowledge. Reason is not just a discourse and a totality of concepts, but a system of operations. (Here again Bastide uses Piaget to move beyond Durkheim). The people of Candomblé have managed to make a transition from a system of collective constraints imposed by the Portuguese to one of inter-mental co-operation. The mythical tradition provided them with frameworks for patterns of thought and behaviour and for new, live social exchanges. Western moderns also have thoughts, behaviour and exchanges, but in their case the mythical tradition behind them is no longer visible. To study their ways scholars must go in the other direction: to find the underlying ideologies behind what is observed. The contemporary Western ethos spells the death of metaphysics or its reduction to the role of simple servant of human interests.

In 1960, aged 62, Bastide passed what was the major and last rite of passage for French academics, the *doctorat d'État.* The dissertation was published (578 pages, excluding the bibliography) under the title *Les religions africaines au Brésil. Contribution à une sociologie des interpénétrations de civilisation*.[17] His jury is star-studded: G. Gurvitch, R. Aron, J. Piaget, A Leroi-Gourhan and H. Gouhier.[18] He receives congratulations, a rare occurrence from juries that included Gurvitch. The study has much wider scope than *Le Candomblé* of 1958. It includes six elements: a history of Africans and of Black religion in Brazil; a theory of religion; an account of social changes from the colonial to the contemporary era; a study of the geographical distribution of African cults; and, finally, a close look at his own specialization, the inter-penetration of civilizations.

While the 1958 book began with a review of the previous Brazilian scholarship, Bastide this time draws a very far-reaching map of the current state of scholarship. He thus presents a summary of the whole social-scientific discussion of religion. He accepts a Marxist view as a starting point: religion is born of the inevitable dimension of failure in human labour and effort, in the struggle against nature and social regimes. But he argues against Marxists who maintain that religion is just an ideology, manipulated by the ruling class pursuing its own interests. He rather sees it arising necessarily out of human misery (a view supported by citations from Karl Marx). With further support from authors as different as Van der Leeuw and Durkheim, he links religion to the sources of energy that humans draw upon for coping with experiences of limits. (A radical empiricist might say that what the mind is good for is to make it possible for humans to survive experience. He might also add that experience may destroy the mind, as *King Lear* shows[19]). To be sure religion is incarnated in the social, but it is not created by it. (Supporting citations from G. Richard). Weber is credited with the determination to understand what religious people do—and what it all means to them. Bastide however warns against the subjectivist turn that looks exclusively at the meaning of the experience for those who have it. Finally he maintains that the search for causal explanations lands scholars into a dead end of little human interest.

Bastide sees a great opportunity for fresh starts in current (French) sociology because of its attentiveness to the diversity of social layers and to shifting situations. (He acknowledges what we might call to the invasion of history into sociology). He also rejoices in the possibilities opened by the sort of ethnology made possible by Lévy-Brühl. Understanding, or explaining other human beings has no value, scientifically or otherwise, if done only with our own categories. The problem of comprehension leads then to an interest in cross-cultural structures, and toward efforts to bring under a common pattern the procedures of different collective representations. Gurvitch is credited with drawing the useful conclusions in his *sociologie en profondeur* and his look at different levels and their constant interaction. From now on, sociologists must think of groups of being as always in a process of structuring and de-structuring. Acculturation and inter-penetration of cultures is therefore the normal state of human affairs, not a rare occurrence limited to a few places of contact.

The history of the scholarly look at Afro-Brazilian cults starts in the late nineteenth century. We hear again of the work of Nina Rodrigues, Oscar Freire, Arthur Ramos and finally Melville Herskovits, who emancipated the study of the trance from the tradition of clinical studies. Gilberto Freyre is praised for overcoming the polemical alteration between the Black and the White points of view. Bastide finds in the history of Brazil both ideological support for an allegedly desirable "whitening" of Brazilian society, and an enduring resistance to the alleged advantages of "whitening" and to the class hierarchies that go with it. Most importantly, marks of fusion, in varying degrees to be sure, are found in all identities. Bastide can thus proceed with the assumption that Afro-Brazilian religion is a live religion with a long history in Brazil and is a factor of adjustment to the overall society. But he is not satisfied with mere functionalism. He wants to see why Candomblé exists, not just why it lasts. To the Black sociologist (Guerreiro Ramos) who proudly stated *niger sum* and added that one must be Black to understand the life of an Afro-Brazilian, Bastide answers that he believes he has undergone the necessary purgation of conceptual clichés. He states, at the beginning of his dissertation, *Africanus sum*; he adds he was initiated into one of the cults he "studied."

A first chapter looks at the arrival of Portuguese and African populations on the coasts of Brazil. The former came with trade in view, but quickly saw the potential for colonization and crops. Sugar cane was the choice, there was a growing market in Europe and the climate was suitable. The cultivation required large estates and much labour. The Indians were deemed unsuitable and the Catholic Church objected to their being reduced to slavery. Estimates of the number of African slaves brought vary; Bastide settles for a total of 3.5 million, adding that numbers increased each century. At the beginning of the nineteenth century, slaves made up the majority of the population in Brazil. At the end of it, their descendants still are the majority, if one includes the numerous mulattos. The slave traffic totally disrupted the religions of the transported Africans. Their culture linked them to family and clan systems, and to specific natural or social environments. Slaves brought with them only such culture as they could carry in their heads and bodies. They were forced to integrate into a new type of society, the *latifundium*, the huge estate owned by a patriarchal family. As mining resources took an increasing share in the overall economy, the traffic in slaves slowed down. Its interruption coincided with the slow advances of the free mulattos and the rise of industrialization. Slavery was abolished in 1888 and new, non-Portuguese, white immigration began shortly afterwards. The big estates became depopulated. A wide range of halfway houses grew between what is conveniently called archaic or colonial and modern Brazil. After the period when Portuguese governors and the Roman Church "governed" the Africans (without pursuing the same objectives), pressures now came from rapid economic changes. African religion secretes, Bastide suggests, protective shells in the new, diverse environments and thus maintains and adapts itself over time. The more sweeping changes come from a shift between the system of patriarchalism and that of competition. In the world Freyre describes in *Casa grande e senzala*, individual mobility is possible for the more fortunate and gifted slaves. The illegitimate mulatto children from the leading white families are emancipated in time. Racial prejudices, as we know them, are few since they are not necessary to maintain threatened barriers: the line between the big house and the slave cabins is here to stay.[20] But in the competition system, when the ex-slaves have to start working for wages, they begin to compete with less dark-skinned Brazilians. They are then kept in the low rungs of the working class ladder. It takes legislation (and enforcement) to deliver some measure of equality.

Afro-Brazilians had recourse to occasional violence. Anger led to burning of sugar fields. A major revolt disturbed Salvador de Bahia in 1835. Assassinations of Whites show no religious component in their motivation. Some Maroons (Black fugitives) organized themselves in bandit bands and their religious practices are quite visible at first. Black fugitives also tried peaceful ways. They started *quilombos*, republics in the hinterland, where they practiced their religion. The most famous and largest of these was Palmares. This attempt was militarily crushed at the end of the seventeenth century. In the *sertao*, Afro-Brazilians of course started mixing with Indians, and this brought about new syncretisms. (Governments tended to stir hatred between Blacks and Indians. In the nineteenth century a regiment of Brazilians with slaves among their ancestors was sent to massacre Indians in the Southwest). In general it became clear very quickly that the rural protests were economic and cultural in nature. With the rise of the system of competition in the cities religious elements fade out more rapidly from the protest movements and political agitation.

In the colonial era, the Catholicism of the Whites and that of the Blacks were quite distinct.[21] Both have more or less the same cycles of feast days. But the Blacks have saints of their own, most notorious San Benedetto (a Moor, not Benedict of Nurcia). And the confraternities are kept entirely distinct. Many African features were tolerated in the festive processions of the Blacks (music, costume dances, street theatre, the crowning of a king). Catholic authorities however suspected ongoing celebration of African gods and strove to purify "religion" from these celebrations and tried to locate them firmly and exclusively in "folklore." The confraternities provided the Black populations with a basis for an active, ongoing social and cultural life. The Blacks offered no resistance to baptism but included their own ceremonies to the funerals, including some animal sacrifice. Blood rituals (roosters and goats) became a source of conflict with clergy and police. Magical practices were tolerated, the Portuguese being as "superstitious" as the Africans. Whites and Indians never failed to get interested in what know-how the Blacks possessed in matters of healing and wish fulfilment. Thus all in all, the Church was not much of an instrument of social control.

A number of African Muslims were brought over as slaves. In Salvador de Bahia their mores remained stricter than those of the Catholics and Muslim instruction lasted a couple of generations. No mosque was built. From an exterior point of view they were Christians, like the others. Their cult slowly disappeared. The name of Allah however survives in some Candomblé hymns.

Bastide concludes his historical part with the putting forward of an idea of counter-acculturation. In spite of the social destruction entailed by forced uprooting, transportation and slavery, resistance occurred, and a new equilibrium was built to replace the variety of lost ones. It remains true that the religion of Candomblé was separated from the daily social life. But the niche became a hiding place and created social forms and hierarchies. The persecutions, sporadic in any case, were ultimately powerless. The invented religion served a function by creating an interior barrier (not unlike saint Teresa of Avila's interior castle). Bastide returned later (in pages 362–396) to problems of syncretism and offered six pages of tables outlining the correspondences between African and Christian figures, regionally differentiated. We speak of syncretism but the African does not need the concept since he does not feel any contradiction. While religion for us is a closed system (consider the role of canonical Scripture and of the *magisterium*), magical thought is a system of accumulation. Africans are in search of an intensification of magical dynamism, to better confront the realities of life. Counter-acculturation is not a return to African civilization, but to a myth of it that the slaves have developed for themselves. Such invented collective "memory" fills unbearable lacunae.

Thus the slaves and their descendants inherited from the colonial era social frameworks for the ongoing practice of an Afro-Brazilian religion in a realistic context. Mystical values were the ones that could not be taken away from them. Gurvitch had defined religion as that which can stand above all social antinomies. Ricoeur argues that religion is where the political meets its limits. The "mystical values" were maintained because the slaves and their descendants survived mentally as well as physically, and because they strove to pursue active individual and social strategies. The army contributed early to the upward mobility of those with slaves in their ancestry. At a more intimate level, slaves and their descendants chose plans of "de-africanization" and whitening of their blood. They could play upon and exploit the fondness for the "Black Venus" shared by many Whites. This interaction in turn "africanized" many Whites.[22] The absence (or weakness)

Syncretism

The Hebrew Bible and the New Testament instruct the faithful to abandon the ways of life of the populations that surround them; many of their practises and their beliefs are viewed as temptations away from the straight and narrow path. Syncretism, i.e. blending or mixing of religions, was for a long time viewed as a dangerous path. In the period of Christian missionary expansion, those who opposed syncretism were ordinarily seen as the more orthodox party. In the beginning of the twentieth century, historians of the Hellenistic world saw that the collapse of the great civic cults of Antiquity made possible the rise of a new religiosity in which individuals became more free to cut an individual path and transform their religion. Syncretism thus emerged slowly as a value-free technical term. But the notion of each religion having an essence kept placing phenomena of acculturation and blending at the margins of the history of the great religions, thereby prolonging the life of the idea that religions are pure entities that can get spoiled.

At the end of the twentieth century the notion became accredited that religions have no (or little) core and no firmly fixed boundaries. Cultures are not stable systems. Syncretism, became viewed as a constant historical process, and one far from being always conscious. Today's orthodoxy may well be yesterday's syncretism. The term hybridation gained currency and served to stress the naturalness of the process. Contemporary scholars consider syncretism a heuristic tool, namely a notion that helps find things out. Leopold and Jensen show that it suggests three lines of inquiry:

1. **Social.** Mixing occurs when groups enter in contact. The mixing usually reflects power relations between them.
2. **Semiotic.** Cultural forms and meanings become known and reinterpreted outside the circles that first shaped them. Humans can change the meaning of their symbols.
3. **Cognitive.** Areas of contact provide new opportunities for mental processes, for revising ways of knowing the environment and adapting to it. Cognitive patterns and needs guide the selection among the newly available processes.

of stigma connected with miscegenation is of course crucial here.

The second part is devoted to the sociology of the contemporary Afro-Brazilian cults. We now hear of sects. The geographical data are first given. We read of the Indians in the North and of the hybrid cults that developed there; then of Recife and the *xangos*, of Bahia and Candomblé. After internal migrations, in the new social context of the South (Rio at first), the

African cults took the form of the *macoumba.* In the new urban, ostensibly egalitarian world, the ideas of the French Allan Kardec, namely spiritism, penetrated into the groups of migrants adhering to the *macoumba*; this led to the new *umbanda* sect. In the South, the sects generally maintain family life, a certain discipline of sexuality, and some degree of economic solidarity. Some sects move toward a political role (the communist party achieved some infiltration). Jorge Amado wrote a novel showing the shift of a young man from Candomblé to unionist militancy. On the whole, it is a "common soul" that is maintained. The emancipated Blacks did not know how to transform themselves into proletarians. Against Durkheim, Bastide stresses that religion in these groups is not just a matter of control or constraint. True the collective representations are there, but also the festive gatherings. Sects are playgroups and friendly associations; networks of complementarities are being built among individuals, a system of gifts and counter-gifts is being maintained.[23] Some of this process remains secret; not all giving and counter-giving is made public.

Bastide observes the appearance of a gap between myths and rituals in these modern circumstances. The collective memory, the oral tradition, is weaker that the motor one. The myths have lost their lyrical wealth and colour. What does not fit the conditions of the new world is forgotten. The myths then tend to become schematic and begin to serve mainly as explanation of rites. This is for Bastide an opportunity to repeat one of his major themes: all groups are always active both in structuring and de-structuring.

Bastide then turns to the disintegration of the cults. In the case of Candomblé, located in what remained of rural parts, Afro-Brazilians being scattered got more deeply integrated into Catholicism, for want of a viable alternative. The few groups that did remain are not objects of much study in his day. It is clear however that rites of initiation have disappeared and that the members of the religious hierarchy have become healers. In the lively urban *macoumba* (in Rio de Janeiro and São Paulo), the division among African nations characteristic of the colonial Candomblé has disappeared. The groups are fluid, and there is much innovation. The ecstasies sometimes turn toward hysteria. Some Whites are attracted. Members of the hierarchy become consultants and have customers, sometimes for black magic. There is an overlap between some groups and criminal gangs.

In the urban conditions of the industrialized South, in a society ideologically committed to egalitarianism, the psychology of resentment developed among some Afro-Brazilians and boosts for self-confidence became sought. (No Christian ethos of patience or belief in the redemptive value of suffering ever got internalized in Brazil.) The case of the *umbanda* is particularly interesting. As we saw above, urban Afro-Brazilians in the South, grouped in the *macoumba*, became interested in the spiritism of Allan Kardec, introduced to Brazilian Whites in 1863 and where it obtained an immediate success. In these original groups only Whites could be guides. But among the Afro-Brazilians, legends about the lost continent of Lemuria, and its "Black" religion which pre-dated the Sanskrit Scriptures, entered into the *umbanda* mix along with the spiritist ideas of contact with souls through mediums. In this process, the African gods were profoundly metamorphosed and the souls of dead slaves became gods who could be called upon to do good. Thus the Blacks could feel that their ancestral beliefs had great moral and modern value. (In fact the values were largely those of occultist movements that were then in fashion with some educated Whites). This Afro-Brazilian assimilation of spiritism was so thorough that the adherents of the *umbanda* religion condemned the "orthodox" *kardecists*. Some messianic expectations and traits are present in the *umbanda*, but Bastide finds no tendency to reject Brazilian national identity. The "spirit of Brazil" is upheld by the *umbandists*; they claim it is the *kardecists* who betray it. (There is thus a big contrast between their messianism and that of African-Americans in the United States). In the old days, he concludes, the images of the saints served as masks for the gods; now the gods serve as masks for the aspirations of a social group bent upon self-improvement and social ascension.[24]

Bastide stresses that the new groups, where all have slaves among their ancestors and all have lighter skins, produced in time a new common cultural possession. *Macumba* and *umbanda* turned into new religions. To try to sort out strands of distinct influences overlooks the unity of the whole. (In sociology, there is no theorem of the composition of forces).[25]

Bastide concludes with a look at the Afro-Brazilians who define themselves as Catholic or Protestant. Since Herskovits, some hold the view that the Blacks reinterpret their Catholicism with the concepts of their older religion. But it must also be seen that Catholicism changed with the separation of Church and State at the end of the nineteenth century. Recruitment of the clergy started among the lower classes, and these clerics struggled against "Negro folklore" with renewed vigour (especially any animal sacrifices offered to the saints). They broke with old plantation usage and let the Blacks enter the church through the main door. The days of two-level Catholicism were over. Afro-Brazilians Protestant converts do not differ much from other converts to the Presbyterian, Methodist and Baptist Churches founded by nineteenth century missionaries. These missionaries were at the front of the Emancipation battles. Their views on conversion, their educational programs and their commitment to schooling tended to cast all members of their fold into the same mould of a scriptural religion of respectability and sobriety.[26] The new illuminist and Pentecostal churches, rapidly growing in the last third of twentieth century, show few colour-related differences. Social integration, a degree of social ascension and increase in self-esteem, are the common and basic phenomena. The sociological here determines the cultural. Bastide's data go up the 1950s. The more recent story has been abundantly researched and the bibliography in Portuguese, French and English is extensive.[27]

The inquiry into inter-penetration of civilizations and that into the relationships between social structures and religious values provide the core matter in the conclusions. In the colonial era, Afro-Brazilians made a distinction between mystical union and demoniacal possession, just like Christian theologians but independently from them. The norms of the Afro-Brazilian religions shape collective consciousness. In a second stage, people who have slaves among their ancestors acquire some of the new "White" ideals of egalitarianism but are placed in a system of competition in which they cannot succeed. It still remains true that the gods make the men. In a third stage, with increasing incorporation in the large society, ecstatic trances shifting toward hysterical crises become indicators of the degree of cohesion or disintegration of the smaller group. The conceptualization of acculturation and counter-acculturation is the most valid guide for these analyses. The study of symbolism keeps a central place on all genuinely sociological study of the inter-penetration of civilizations.

The concepts of collective memory and of cultural reproduction are also central. Attention is paid to the links between social phenomena and objects, social structure and daily life. It is a rule that social matter is always "culturalized" and exists only in so far as social agents give it some signification in terms of their symbolic capital. Social structures make it possible for values to function, to be actualized in co-ordinated actions and lead thereby to shared meanings. These generalizations, thinks Bastide, can serve for the study of all Afro-American religions, from the Argentine to the US South.

The expectations and life plans of Afro-Brazilians changed with the economic, social and political circumstances. After finding cohesion in remaining religiously distinct, they sought it in joining the whole (to varying degrees of course). At this historical point any community sharing values tends to oscillate between focussing on the sacred or on developing an ideology. The Brazilian history shows a constant compromise between both. The distinctiveness of religion is that its values lend meaning to reality, whereas the values of ideology give expression to the interests or frustrations of a social group. Some ideologies are quite religious and they cannot completely erase the distinctive characteristic of the sacred. Sociologists must acknowledge that such movements cannot be entirely assimilated to political ones.

In 1972, two years before his death, Bastide helped prepare a collection of Portuguese articles on Afro-Brazilian literature and religions and wrote his only retrospective and autobiographical piece.[28] He attests that paying attention to Candomblé occasioned an intellectual crisis: his mental equipment, focussing on spotting contradictions, was not appropriate. He therefore had to get "converted" to another mentality. It became clear to him that pure thought does not exist. His thinking could not remain coloured by the requirements of his French culture. So he could not just look outside; he had to get inside. This process led in his case to a durable sort of personal enchantment. The most clear scholarly result is the affirmation that there is an African metaphysics. His subsequent work on African anthropology confirmed it (along with that of others). Over the centuries of Western thought, language became wedded to a metaphysics, which is not that of the Africans.

As we shall see, Bastide's work has been epoch-making in the study of Afro-Brazilian religions. It also spawned studies on religious acculturation in Africa. And it remains of enduring interest for all attempts at theorizing religion, and this for three reasons.

1. His sociology of religion is historically informed. Portugal, Spain, France and England were different to start with and it does not get us very far to point out that the last one was Protestant and the first three Catholic, since their Catholicisms were different in very significant ways. New Portugal was not New Spain, New France, or New England. The interests and cultures of the Europeans who crossed the ocean were different, and so were the geographies they settled in. So also were different the populations they met (invaded?) and the manner of the cohabitation they got into.
2. The core of his method is sociological but reoriented by the simultaneous advances in ethnology. His sociology is therefore completely contextualized. This results from Mauss's notion of total social fact. Also from the attention Gurvitch paid to different layers and levels of interaction. An account of religion needs to go into matters of folklore (e.g. cooking and the hunting of lice), interpersonal relations (e.g. sexuality), economics, art, and politics. The list can be extended and become more detailed.

3. His theory of religion centres itself on the issue of live time, on the matters of memory and expectation, on the concern to keep living throughout the generations and live as well as possible. Cultural and social reproduction is a problem modern Frenchmen face as well as transported African slaves. Since he acknowledged that, the path he opened was not just that of scientific progress but included a personal enrichment. (Should we speak of spiritual growth?)

During the years of World War II, before the decades of decolonization, Bastide laid the basis for understanding why so called "inferior" people, weakened under the impact of "stronger" people, do not let themselves die. He also laid the basis for seeing how they go about surviving and remaining themselves. To make these points in 1945 was reversing a trend. At the end of the nineteenth century, a New Zealand statesman arguing for the legislation that would set aside some land for the Maoris, saw it as measure of relief, just like the gesture of a compassionate nurse putting a pillow under the head of a dying man. In an intellectual autobiography, Marshall Sahlins, the Chicago anthropologist, recalls what he learned during the years of his commitment against the war in Vietnam, and writes that the dominant theory in anthropology at the time was that indigenous people who do not assimilate the ways of the expansionist West, are doomed to a life of "dependency and despondency." [29] (Sahlins became the historian of the response of the Polynesian natives to the contact with the British and Americans). The Maoris are still with us and the history of African slaves transported to the New World is now shown to be also a record of courage and resiliency. They had some freedom at a certain level and used it to persist in the expression of their own cultural singularity.

Chapter 6

The Paris career: The world of French ethnologists

From 1954 until his retirement in 1968 Bastide was professor at the Sorbonne in Paris. (He returned to Brazil for extended stays in 1962 and 1973). His chair, was named "Ethnologie sociale et religieuse," the designation to which Lévy-Brühl had given currency. His activities were numerous and his production intense. In touch with French Africanists, he assimilated the results of their research, did field work in Africa, and wrote on a group of Afro-Brazilians who returned to Africa.[1] This chapter will focus on his general institutional involvements. Specific developments in theory of religion will be examined in the next chapters.

In the first two years Bastide wrote his dissertation and his book on Candomblé. He then produced a variety of books that share a somewhat different profile. They reflect his teaching, and opened up new areas of sociology; they have a sort of textbook quality, reflecting the current state of specific questions (with abundant international bibliography) and seem intended for gifted undergraduates. In this vein are *Sociologie des maladies mentales* (1965; English translation in 1972), *Les Amériques noires* (1967, 1973, 1996),[2] and *Anthropologie appliquée* (1971; English 1973). In this category I would also place *Sociologie et psychanalyse*, first published in Portuguese in 1948 (1950, 1972, 1995). Many of these books were translated into a range of languages.

Bastide also co-operated in a number of joint ventures. Gurvitch asked him to contribute three articles to his two volumes *Traité de sociologie* (1960). He wrote "Sociologie et psychologie"[3] "Problèmes de l'entrecroisement des civilisations et de leurs oeuvres,"[4] "Sociologie et psychanalyse."[5] He wrote many articles in the *Encyclopaedia Universalis,* the French equivalent of the Britannica, including: "Acculturation", "Anthropologie religieuse," "Initiation," "Intériorité et subjectivité," "Magie," "Sacrifice," and "Utopie." He also contributed articles to *Ethnologie générale,* a multiauthored encyclopaedia on ethnology, most noteworthy among them being "Mythologie."[6] He also made a contribution to a collection of articles, *Introduction aux sciences humaines des religions.*[7] (This important piece will receive a detailed examination later.) His contribution to the multi-volume *Histoire des religions*[8] appeared posthumously.

His research took place in research centres, which were also training grounds for graduate students. In 1959 he founded a Centre of Social Psychiatry, where he directed a seminar. In 1965, upon the death of Gurvitch, he succeeded him as director of the Centre for Sociology of Knowledge. He was also an assiduous presence at a variety of international conferences. The bio-bibliography prepared by Claude Ravelet indicates three or four of them every year, and his contributions are scattered in a variety of *Proceedings*.

Once in Paris, he came into close contact with the younger generation of French ethnologists. The first to be mentioned is Pierre Verger, whom he had already met in Brazil when Verger was having a career as a photographer. He introduced him to Afro-Brazilians and this gave Verger a fresh impetus for his work.

Pierre Verger (1902–1996)

At the age of thirty, Verger abandoned a conventional life in a conventional milieu, seized as he was by his passion for taking pictures and travelling. He became one of the great photographers of the twentieth century. He quickly succeeded in making a living with his camera. Working with the *Musée d'Ethnographie* in Paris he started to bridge the gap between the pictures as "scientific documents" gathered by anthropologists and the works of art shown in galleries.

When he was in Brazil in 1946, Bastide urged him to go to Salvador de Bahia and introduced him to Afro-Brazilians and their lives. Verger's life then took a new turn. He became the indefatigable photographer of the everyday life of the descendants of African slaves living in the Americas; his collections are particularly rich for Brazil, Cuba and Haiti. He travelled extensively in French Africa. Théodore Monod, Head of the *Institut français d'Afrique Noire*, saw two thousand of his pictures and persuaded him to write on what he saw. Verger thus began a new career as scientific writer. He left important work on the plants and medicine of the Yoruba. Above all he drew attention to the constant traffic between and Bahia and the coast of Africa. In 1958 he invited Bastide to Dahomey and introduced him to the Afro-brazilians who had returned to Africa. Verger and Bastide kept up a rich correspondence and Bastide wrote a preface to his book on African gods. Verger was initiated in the religion of the Yoruba. He spent the last years of his life in Salvador de Bahia. Many of his publications (texts and photo albums) are in Portuguese. The Fondation Pierre Verger holds his rich archives and 5500 of his photos are available on the site of the Foundation.

Michel Leiris (1901–1990)

This Parisian was first of all a writer, poet and essayist. He was an active participant in the surrealist movement from 1924 to 1929. To become an ethnologist was clearly for him a way to shake off his acquired culture. He was one of the first students of Maurice Leenhardt and became a life-long friend of his contemporary Alfred Métraux. Both shared an interest in possession cults. Leiris wrote on its Ethiopian form; he describes possession liturgies as living theatre. He is known for having said he was he would prefer being possessed to studying possessed people.

He and Métraux come to their ethnographic fields as "passionate" spectators. A gap remained between them and the indigenous people who were caught up by the trance, but these ethnologists derived comfort (as well as material for science) from the realization that some fellow humans can know this sort of life. Both his literary output and his scholarly writing derived from an attempt to understand the "whole human being." He has been compared to Montaigne.

In Paris Bastide also met Michel Leiris, a man of letters who had been part of Griaule's research team in Africa. Like Verger, Leiris was an artist, perhaps primarily so. He had arrived late to ethnographic studies.

This rhythm of activities was maintained in the years after his retirement until his death in 1974. In 1971 he moved to Québec where he taught at the Université de Sherbrooke with Henri Desroche. Here too he made a decisive contribution to the training of several graduate students. The activities of his 1973 trip to São Paulo, where he planned to write on developments on Afro-Brazilian religions since 1960, were slowed down due to worsening health conditions.

In an important article on the history of ethnological studies, Jean Duvignaud, who was one of his students, begins by affirming that the West has probably been of all the great civilizations the one that remained most blind to the realities lived by the populations and civilizations it encountered in the course of its history. Their medieval writings certainly compare very unfavourably with those of the Muslim travellers of the same period.[9] He also stresses that the generation of researchers active in France since the 1930s shared the conviction that the world was being changed before their eyes in an irreversible manner. This forced them to take stock of where their own lives were going, thus imposing the tasks of an auto-anthropology. We can now understand their commitment to aesthetic creation, to literary modes of expression and other artistic endeavours. Verger and Leiris are only two of the authors who realized that the old clichés of exoticism were just part of an ancient tradition of blindness.[10]

Some of this generation of ethnologists occupied distinguished University positions. Métraux is one of them but he too travelled to release the hold

Alfred Métraux (1902–1963)

This Swiss-born anthropologist has been said to be in the line of the European travellers, walking in the footsteps of Herodotus, in search of understanding different civilizations. He was also an academic and wrote a thesis on a South American Indian tribe, the Tupi Guarani, and acquired a wide expertise on neighbouring tribes as well. He went to Easter Island and Haiti and wrote on both. His best-known work is on Haitian Voodoo and its rituals of possession (1958). He showed how this religion, adapted from Africa, played a role in the political movement that led to the Haitian War of Independence (1791). He described the social organization of Voodoo, its view of the supernatural world, its rituals and its relationships to magic and witchcraft. He also showed how the 1884 book by Sir Spencer St John created the legend about the cruelty and filth of this religion. From 1939 the Catholic Church undertook in earnest to eradicate the cult but, even with the support of the State, it did not manage to do away with the notion that one can be both Catholic and a practitioner of Voodoo. In contrast Protestants obtained conversions by assuring that their faith was a refuge from Voodoo. Pentecostal churches include trances in their liturgy. Métraux and Bastide thus laid together the basis for contrasting the two major Afro-American religions.

From 1938 Métraux taught at Berkeley and Yale. After 1950 he led the UNESCO anti-racism programme and taught at the École Pratique des Hautes Études in Paris.

His friend Michel Leiris told how one night, while both were walking in the streets of Port-au-Prince, Métraux talked of his search for a solution to what was to him a haunting poetic and scholarly problem: how to write for others about the singular realities he saw, about what he experienced and enjoyed. Leiris added that under the appearance of a prim and Protestant professor was hidden a deep interest for the burlesque, and sudden, passionate movements.

upon himself of his own native culture; he opened himself to other cultures in search of an ability to somewhat change himself. His publications are impeccably scientific but they do show an affectionate relationship to the people he observed.

Métraux, while a highly specialized scholar, joined the Social Sciences Department of UNESCO in 1950 and orchestrated a series of studies on racism, which were published in the journal *Le racisme devant la science* published since 1951. Bastide's involvement in this public interest work completes the picture of the scholar by showing a dimension of international public service. He did not hesitate to see in the world-wide combat against racism the one victory to be gained if genuine international development was to become possible. He repeated his conviction that cultures do not develop by self-fecundation but by inter-fecundation.[11] Lévi-Strauss was also recruited for the work, but his contribution caused a controversy.

To the vast project of public education, Bastide contributed his survey of *Les Amériques Noires. Les civilisations africaines dans le Nouveau Monde.*[12] In 236 pages he presents, within a thematic framework, the diversity of the histories and social conditions of populations of African origin, from Argentina to the United States. He covers Brazil, Peru, Bolivia, Colombia, Venezuela, the three Guyanas, Honduras, Panama, Mexico, the British and the French West Indies, Cuba, the Dominican Republic, Haiti and Puerto-Rico. He keeps on with his project of contextualising the study of religion. He discusses economics, folklore, family relations, social organization, religion, and general race relations. The sociological approach ensures that the colour of the skin becomes only one of many important factors. Every time local history and socio-economic conditions are seen as transforming this "world of Blacks" into a world of groups with very different cultures, aspirations and prospects. He concludes with an account of the many movements seeking to revive and promote *négritude,* namely forms of Black pride, with Markus Garvey (United States) and Aimé Césaire (Martinique). Stokely Carmichael (born in Trinidad) is not included. His famous *Black Power* speech was spoken a few months before the publication of Bastide's book.

The collection *Le prochain et le lointain* includes a couple of detailed studies written in this context. A 1965 article (part of a UNESCO spon-

Claude Lévi-Strauss on race

In 1971 UNESCO organized an international year of struggle against racism and asked Lévi-Strauss to give the inaugural conference. (He had published twenty years before a text entitled *Race and culture*). Rather than repeat what he had already said, he wrote a new address. Wanting to be frank and timely, he began by saying that there was nothing more to be learned along the lines of the old physical anthropology (skull measurements etc.) but that recent developments in genetics promised important scientific data, even though no laws were about to be enunciated. Then he moved on to his main topic. The diversity of cultures, he argued, is real and important enough even though it cannot be traced to alleged "racial" differences or to different genes. Every civilization cultivates its own specific differences; cultures, not genes or skin colour, firm up the differentiations. In an ideal situation, cultures stimulate each other and do not obliterate their differences. Groups do want to have some hold upon their future. Overlooking this serious resolve, he continued, may well be responsible for the small results achieved in the fight against what is commonly called racism. He concluded that the blanket denunciation of "prejudices" is not likely to stop the growing degrees of intolerance, which he saw on the horizon.

The UNESCO establishment did not welcome this challenge to its anti-racism optimism and simple de-colonization dogmas. Lévi-Strauss later narrated how his reading of his text was sabotaged by the chair in the plenary assembly.

sored study, originally published in English)[13] entitled "Les effets de l'industrialisation sur les relations raciales au Brésil" shows how the European immigrants on the whole adopted the Luso-Brazilian mentality where numerous compensatory and alleviating mechanisms blurred the realities of colour-based domination. Blacks enter the proletariat at the lowest rung, namely the construction industry, and slowly climb up the ladder thanks to labour legislation.[14]

A further UNESCO-sponsored study (unfortunately interrupted) examined "Stéréotypes, normes et comportement racial à São Paulo, Brésil"[15] and strove to grasp the forms of prejudice specific to this population. Questionnaires and statistical analyses establish, for instance, that 55% of Whites consider the Blacks to be of "equal intelligence." Discrimination appears in a class when it feels threatened with "invasion" by people who have slaves among their ancestors. But in the end he acknowledges the questionnaires were not designed carefully enough, so that the specific form of "the Brazilian dilemma" remains elusive.

Most significant, I think, is the long introduction Bastide wrote for the French publication of *A Rap on Race* published in New York in 1971 by Margaret Mead and James Baldwin. The two protagonists met in Paris, started talking and ended up spending seven hours in the next three days pursuing the exchange while being recorded on tape. Thus the book was born. Bastide encouraged a prompt French translation; he knew Margaret Mead, having met her during her trip to São Paulo.[16] He found the dialogue exemplary but, unfortunately, not representative. He presents it not as a meeting of two races, but as a moment of history.

He begins with a sketch of the two conversationalists. Margaret Mead is an anthropologist with a very distinguished record of work in Samoa and New Guinea. She is the leading figure in the school of "culture and personality," keen to see the way different cultures foster different types of personality formation. Attentive from the start to the condition of women in her home country, she is resolved to bring about change in it. Baldwin, a writer, discovered he could not affirm himself freely as Black in a world of hostile US Whites. He went to France where he discovered he was an American rather than a Black, and that this condition was more comfortable. Both Mead and Baldwin agree that social integration should be the goal in the US but that this cannot be done without deep changes in values and in institutions. (So both are situated between the older well-meaning liberal Whites and the new generation of Black separatists). Both are critical of the land of their birth, and both were changed by living in another world.

While Mead is reformist, Baldwin is more revolutionary. But they do not just talk ideas; they also share a will to bring about change. Margaret Mead sees her task as an anthropologist as "inventing the future." They agree on the rift between the Black bourgeoisie that succeeded in America by adopting the values of the White middle class, and the rest of the Blacks who remain mired in poverty and keep Black ways. They see the point made by Stokely Carmichael, namely that Blacks should cease to count on support and leadership from good Whites and aim at Black Power.

Bastide clearly sees that the two conversationalists do not view integration in the same manner. Equality between Whites and Blacks does not challenge Margaret Mead's values, since she is an individualist who accepts responsibility for what she does but only that. She had nothing to do with the decision to drop the atom bomb on Hiroshima; she is not responsible for the transportation of slaves. She refuses to be the captive of the dead and of what they did. She acts here and now. But Baldwin, like his African ancestors, is communitarian. He cannot so easily ignore or reject the past of his people. His person does not exist without participation in a collective, in his people, and in their shared history. Baldwin is not a proponent of some reinvented *négritude* or return to Africa. It is only the US dominant ideology of forced severance from the Old World that he rejects for his New World. Margaret Mead and James Baldwin engage themselves in an exemplary dialogue because they are sad for the country of their birth and challenge its ways. This helps them talk. But their disquiet is not the same.

In the end Bastide sides with Baldwin. His final pages make proposals for Frenchmen and stress that they must learn to see the difference between Blacks raised in their former African colonies and Blacks from the French Caribbean islands, who are fellow citizens. As always, he draws attention to persistent singularities.

In his 1972 retrospective text Bastide states that his study of racial relations has always tried to be attentive to the revolts present in the voice and actions of the victims of racial oppression.[17] In 1940 and 1941 he had published a series of studies on successive generations of Afro-Brazilian poets, most notably Cruz e Souza, a late nineteenth century author, who was working within the French Parnassian and Symbolist schools.[18] Bastide discerned in his poems something African hidden under the conventions of the high poetic tradition. But a Brazilian literary critic objected to this guesswork: Cruz e Sousa was in his eyes an obvious follower of Mallarmé. This is all that needs to be said. Bastide however quotes Bachelard: "there is science only of the hidden." He also invokes Freud and his notion of "convergences" that give some unmistakable if elusive message. Can there be any penetrating insight without looking further than what meets the eye? Cruz e Souza may well have wanted to be aryanized but, as he himself puts it, if he wanted to make a white music, his ancestors' tam-tam kept beating inside him. Experienced study of race relations must keep an ear for the social struggles and the hidden angers. Bastide's literary culture makes him especially sensitive to the tremors that real life conflicts communicate to the language of the poet.

Chapter 7

Leaving safe ground: Acknowledging the fluidity of human interaction

Between 1970 and 1973 Bastide published three collections of previously published articles along with some new materials. The three titles *Le prochain et le lointain* (1970), *Le Rêve, la transe et la folie* (1972), *Estudos afro-brasileiros* (1973)[1] give us the farthest points reached in his thinking and writing. All examine, in some way or other, what happens when individuals and groups leave the ground of their familiar truths to get on alien grounds, far from group security and the presence of only well-known evils.[2] Here we shall focus mainly on the texts that enable us to focus on the theory of religion that emerged from his specialized work. The general focus in his theorizing of religion runs along the lines of common concerns that took shape in his day. I can borrow a definition from Charles Long, the US historian of religion who has done most to further studies on the religion of Black Americans. Religion, he writes, is "how one comes to terms with the ultimate significance of one's place in the world." I see a convergence between this definition and two points essential to Bastide's work: people need to have "a place in the world" and they must actively "come to terms" with it.[3]

"Calvinisme et racisme"[4] take us to grounds much ploughed since Weber's *Protestant Ethic*, namely that of the cultural by-products of the doctrine and ethics at the heart of Calvinist churches. The doctrine of predestination, as found in the works of Augustine, Luther and Calvin, seemed in these churches to transform the dark secrets of the divine will into some luminous behaviour. God, like Jeremiah's potter, works on mankind as on clay, and rejects some of the pots he shaped for reasons known only to himself.[5] A terrible metaphor, which gave rise to a frightful doctrine, that of double predestination, a dark abyss into which most theologians prefer not to gaze. The immediate context of Bastide's 1958 article is the embarrassment in the World Council of Churches before the defence of apartheid put forward by the Dutch Reformed Church of South Africa. So he raises the question: is there a link between Protestantism and racial prejudice? Are Calvinists quick to shift from the honour of God to the pride of his chosen people? It is well known that New England Puritans made high demands on the Indians before they could be considered "regenerated" and that they, on the whole, preferred not to mix with them (unlike the Portuguese or the French). Did the difficulties of missionary work lead then into racism? In the nineteenth century, Sierra Leone was born of white humanitarian and Christian efforts to find an alternative to slavery. Here again failure led to disenchantment about the race Protestants had tried so hard to "redeem."

Having posed the problem, Bastide examines Calvin's texts. All humans are equally capable of knowing God; all are equally under the sway of sin. The elect sever themselves from the world of sinful splendour and enjoyments; and this little group values itself highly. But Calvin never affirmed Christians could tell who was saved and who was damned. The visible church is a historical group charged with the task of announcing the Gospel to all. It is not to be confused with the invisible (or mystical) gathering of the elect. Under the novel conditions of the sixteenth century, Calvin makes of the visible church a society of people bound by a contract. There is no racism here. So Bastide turns to a better question: can this ecclesiology provide, after the fact, a justification for a racism born subsequently from different causes?

Racial relations in the modern world, he proposes, have been cast within one of two moulds: the patriarchal one and the competitive one. In the first model, the dominant minority derives huge benefits and has a protective attitude; racially mixed births are frequent. Racial prejudice as such is unnecessary since the ethos and power structure are stable. In the second competitive world, racial mixing is prohibited or severely limited on ostensibly moral grounds; economic competition is feared and racial prejudice both rampant and powerful. Can one isolate the Calvinist variable in the constitution of the second model? Bastide doubts it and refers to contemporary US studies that failed to show Protestants being more prejudiced than their fellow citizens. "Situation" is the cause more than "religion."

Bastide looks at specific cases. The Dutch controlled Northeast Brazil from 1630 to 1661 and operated the economic system of sugar plantations the Portuguese had started. They disapproved of slavery, introduced the Bible to the Afro-Brazilians and were determined to curb debauchery and emancipate converted slaves. They clearly acted on their principles. But the economic context proved stronger than the religion. "Sugar cannot be produced without African slaves." In Cape Town the Dutch and

French Calvinists were at first merchants, soldiers and a few settlers. Single men cohabited with native women. The Dutch farmers in the interior, all with wives and children, had a policy of separation from the natives and paternalistic policies with their African servants and slaves. They gave them earnest religious education and emancipated those who had progressed on the path to salvation. When the British conquered South Africa, the conflict between the new comers and the Boer was not religious, but political and economic. (Mining and industrialization became the dominant economic realities controlled by the British). The Boer defended their rural way of life against the new competitive economy that needed salaried Black workers. Their strategy won at the (Whites only) polls and the Boer started to implement their theory of separate development, thereby claiming to enable both their own way of life (as an embattled minority) and that of the Bantus to evolve in continuity with their respective past. The Bible was quoted as sanctifying cultural diversity rather than abolishing it. Apartheid, in these terms, was not a means of racial exploitation. The worm however was in the fruit. While the theologians wanted to protect distinct community identities, the political power saw to it that the State gave all the good land to the Whites.

Bastide can point out that the Boer, with their Bible, had pretty much the same outlook as the Portuguese Jesuits with their saints. And he adds that US racists who want to keep the Negroes in their place, defend economic interests and protect themselves from what they see as threats to their morality. There may be some Calvinism in that, but what is proved by the historically informed analyses is that Calvinism "plays" differently according to the situations and produces different cultural and social consequences. What matters is not how Calvinists tried to fathom their status as elect, since they accepted it with thanksgiving, but how they lived it, under the circumstances.

The role of circumstances looms large again in the case of folklore and its shifting lines of differentiation from religion.[6] Contrary to what nineteenth century folklorists did, confronted, as they thought they were, with "dying" European folklore, folklore in Bastide's generation started being studied in the full context of the lived realities that surround it. The case of Brazil offered a perfect illustration. The rituals of the summer equinox, the feast of Saint John, has trouble keeping its associations when June 24 is the first day of winter; likewise for Christmas, when it comes in the hottest days of the year. Agricultural rituals need to find new saints to sponsor them since seeding and harvest time have moved to different dates in the calendar. The exuberant fires of the Saint John festival remain in the Summer solstice but this is December 24, not June 24. Another innovation

Henri Desroche (1914–1994)

Desroche published on the Shakers and on the Kibbutz. He also wrote on the nineteenth century authors of utopias. His work led him to sharpen his interest in Marxism. He left the Church in 1949 and pursued the exploration of utopian socialisms and of what he called "religions of contraband," namely those European groups, mainly Protestant, who protested on both religious and social grounds and attempted to found alternate societies. (He thus added a nice new turn of phrase to his earlier one of sociology of hope). In European *Ancien Régime* and in British India the State attempted to monopolize the sale of salt and derived income from the practice. Salt became the major item of contraband and the enforcing of the law on salt became a key move to support the political regime.

A major achievement was his directing of a big dictionary of messianisms: *Dieux d'hommes. Dictionnaire des messianismes et millénarismes de l'Ère chrétienne.* Movements in five continents are repertoried; the collection lays the basis for what Desroche liked to call the sociology of hope.

Desroche published on co-operative movements. He entered the fray on theories of development, which were then in heated discussion, and often dominated by simple-minded economists. From 1956 to 1980 he was director of the *Archives de Sciences Sociales des Religions*. After Bastide's death, Desroche organized the publication of homages to his friend and was the major energy behind the founding of the review *Bastidiana.*

appears: the Christmas crib gets thrown into the fire. A new feast, a shifting one, the feast of the Holy Spirit marks the end of winter in late August or September. The Portuguese tried to take their nymphs, ogres and dragons with them, but with small success, since the land was already mapped by an indigenous "sacred" geography. The new markers were accepted, but lost their religious quality to become folklore. Both Indians and Portuguese lost some collective memories in the process. The Jesuits industriously assembled a syncretistic folklore, hoping to construct a gateway to the Faith for Indians and Afro-Brazilians alike. But the Jesuits remained on the coast, and their institutions lasted only as long as social groups accepted them, usually trade corporations or African "nations." Inland, the plantation chaplains were not so proactive. In between the priests' rare visits, inland communities developed their own prayers and vows—and their own lay leadership (from which ranks rose the leaders of the messianic movements). The Church's creations in the coastal cities, born of compromise, lasted because leading citizens maintained their social rank by supporting them. As the influence of these people waned, the *carnaval*, a more recent invention, which does not herald Spring but announces the end of Summer, provided outbursts of jollity and became the enduring refuge of folklore. In time it served as means of integrating the new immigrants.

The new calendar rhythms that crystallized in Brazil show a constant shifting between religious and non-religious folkloric motifs. Clearly some definition of religion is underlying in these pages. But it is not explicit in this 1950 article.

A last section in the 1970 book offers articles dealing with messianism and millenarism, topics that attracted at that time the attention of anthropologists everywhere and of historians of colonialism. The whole collection is dedicated to Henri Desroche, former member of the Dominican order, who had embarked upon the study of those early modern sectarian movements that succeeded in giving shape to utopian communities. When Bastide arrived in Paris he quickly found that the two of them had much in common. They both liked finding what is on the other side of the border; both were keen to find the link between instituting religious experiences and instituted realities. They kept searching, in a variety of cultures, what happens when dreams and utopias move beyond the spontaneous festive state and create durable institutions.

With the essays on messianisms, the student of religion, often focused on religious normalcy, is taken to unfamiliar grounds and extreme behaviours. In these cases the familiar line drawn between those who believe and those who don't, becomes the separation between those who are caught in the frenzy and the scholars who see the whole thing as pathological and bound to lead to nefarious and ultimately self-destructive courses of action. One article examines the alleged connection between famines and messianic turmoil in Brazil. The evidence, Bastide proposes, does not allow the drawing of conclusions about a direct determinative action. Links however are visible between the rise of *cangaceiros* (groups of desperate and murderous bandits with a high sense of their honour), and the "fanatical pilgrims" that drew crowds on their marches guided by messianic expectations. Food deprivation, in some cases encouraged by fasting, very probably entered into the production of visions but is not enough to provide a sufficient account for the whole phenomenon. Two further factors are required: a mythology giving shape to expectations and a sense that a political solution is impossible.[7] Another article reviews the available stories of individuals caught in failed messianic movements. Afro-Brazilians are absent among the leaders of such movements, a salient fact since Black messianisms are found in the US and in Africa. Messianic leaders in Brazil are unfailingly *cabocles*, Indians or Brazilians that have an Indian ancestor, who see all political avenues closed before them. A few Afro-Brazilians are found among the followers of these messianic leaders. Is it that they are frustrated enough to entertain messianic fantasies but not desperate enough to create them? Or is there a missing ingredient? Such as something related to a difference in religious culture?

A theoretically important article shows that since Auguste Comte utopias are no longer considered as socially irrelevant products of the imagination and an unfailing source of errors and illusions.[8] Their creative value and energizing qualities become acknowledged by sociologists. A similar rehabilitation occurred in the case of myth. Bastide reviews the work of Karl Mannheim, George Sorel, Maurice Leenhardt and Mircea Eliade.[9] While these authors agree on the socially powerful role of imagination, some celebrate the power exercised by myth from the past, while others laud the power of utopia for the future. Not surprisingly, Bastide turns to considerations from sociology of knowledge and links mental structures to social ones. Myth "transforms history into nature"[10] and reason is originally happy to do its work within such framework.

But the differentiation of groups and the rise of individualism give birth to myths that are no longer nourished by the larger society and can no longer resist the pressures from the individual unconscious and the dreams of the libido. Individuals and groups can then bend old mythical thinking to their own needs.[11] It is in such context that utopias arise with their views of Earth about to be liberated from Evil. Utopias become ideologies in the strict sense of the term, and stir the hope of unanimous action and nourish political actions to restore the Good Society. Messianism then is an intermediate form, at the middle of a spectrum between myth at one end and utopia at the other. Myths of Creation and of the Civilizing Hero become transformed into myths of the Apocalypse and of the Liberating Hero.

A 1961 article handles the topic in the context of the interest, among international officialdom, for theories of development. (Such interest was then growing rapidly). Do religions help or hinder development? Of course all the sociologist can do with such a question is examine possible links between certain forms of religion and equally specific forms of development. Marx and Engels looked at older European millenarisms and gave an ambivalent testimony. Is messianism the only possible form of resistance in some dire cases? Or is it a misdirection of energy away from material struggles? George Balandier convinced French social scientists that modern African messianic movements must be studied from the point of view of the colonized people, not of the colonial administrators. The work of A. Wallace on the North American Indians and of P. Worsley on the Pacific Cargo cults also accomplished such a shift.[12] So did Lanternari with his *Religion of the Oppressed*.[13] At the very least, messianisms in the colonial world must be viewed as a crisis of growth, a first engagement on the way of cultural transformation. But historical differences must not be overlooked. There are at least three kinds of messianisms, colonial, folk

Bastide on mythology

In the course of the nineteenth century scholars undertook to find the source of mythology in the depths of human nature. Two important steps launched research on promising tracks. Andrew Lang compared what was being found about the mythologies of people called primitives (i.e. populations that did not write) and the Greek mythology that Westerners were familiar with—and had been produced by what was considered gifted people and a source of European civilization. Then it was increasingly allowed that mythology belongs to the world of art and aesthetics as well as of religion. A corollary was that religion could not live without imagination.

Bastide wrote that the essence of mythology lies in being a work of the imagination "an interweaving of explanations of natural phenomena, entertaining tales and heroic legends, thus a creation of poets and historians." Twentieth century ethnology collected mythologies of numerous cultures—and usually gave up the attempt to find the root cause of them all. But they did document the fact that mythologies were the earliest visible ordering of the world; some even spoke of the earliest form of science. This scholarship led to a rehabilitation of the mental capacities of "primitives." Lévi-Strauss studied the mythologies of American Indians as a structuralist and found in them the basic patterns of the mental ordering of the world.

Bastide affirms also a link between mythologies and temporality. Concepts claim to be valid for all times. Myths tell a sequence of events, a story. There is a corollary to this. Everything that happens tends to the mythical. Mythologies "circumscribe" events, and translate them into the language of meaning. Finally Bastide stresses that myths can be both conceived and lived. In the first case, they have become stories, transmitted narrative. These are the objects of structuralist analyses. But before being congealed in this way, speaking mythically was a live activity of the whole human being. This is what Bastide seeks to understand in his "religious ethnology."

and urban. They are all adaptive but work different adaptations. Messianic movements are always two-sided: one side is energizing, the other prefers dreams to effort. And many, in fact, turned into sects, namely groups that break with the world and cultivate a way of thinking that always gives the same answers despite of the fact that the questions change. Social scientists have their blindness too. The difficulty that invaded populations have of adjusting ancient values to new needs is often undervalued among them. It is the old question of the new wine in old wineskins. Theories of development circulating in internationalist circles are much too sweeping in their ambitions. (They illustrate the Promethean identity of which Gurvitch spoke).[14]

A final article looks at the few examples of Portuguese messianic movements in the colonial world, and the more numerous Spanish ones. A few Spanish Dominicans opposed their fantastic visions to the scholastic arguments of Las Casas who was defending the interests of the Indians. Thus the visionaries justified war against the Indians, considered to be an apostate tribe of Israel. Father Francisco de La Cruz went as far as justifying polygamy for Whites to increase Christian population in the New World. He also prophesied the destruction of corrupt Europe and the return of Christ in the New World, in Peru more precisely.[15] The germs of South American hispanophone nationalism lie hidden in such revelations. A later version of it, the Indianism of the early nineteenth century, celebrated the Latin American connection with the Indian the better to sever connections with Spain. Such nationalism was at the time the work of intellectuals. In South America, the State existed before the Nation.

In each of the three parts (race relations, acculturation, messianisms) *Le prochain et le lointain* leaves the neighbour (biblical echo here) to move toward the distant people. It demonstrates the fragility of apparently solid home made thinking, and its inability to handle the wide world of human diversity. It invites to an intellectual life busy in contact places; it commends the crossing of borders, the becoming attentive to others. And it stresses the fluidity of all patterns of human interaction.

The same sense of fragility of acquired truths is at the centre of the second collection of articles *Le rêve, la transe et la folie,* which focus on the area where psychology and ethnology overlap. The three words in the title designate realities that the "primitives" see connected and which moderns consider entirely distinct.

The collection of articles on dreams begins with some early pieces, mainly programmatic and offering only fragmentary data. Bastide objects to the view of Halbwachs, who argued (influenced by Bergson on this point) that humans are socialized when awake but elaborate pure fantasies when asleep. So he sides with Freud, who started with the hypothesis that society is active in us even when we sleep. But Freud did not complete the job: after re-personalizing dreams, they must be re-socialized.[16] This said, Bastide deplores the fact that most studies on dreams forget the dreamers and their concrete social insertion, just like early folklorists showed no interest for the tellers of tales they fondly collected. The time has therefore come for a sociological look at dreams. A 1970 conference *Rêve et culture* advances firmly: primitives consider sleep as a time of more intense life, while moderns tend to think of dreams as dross or garbage. Moderns seem to have all gone to Marx's school and consider work to be the essence of life; most link the life of reason to techniques of productivity. What then are dreams for? Freud gives us an acceptable answer: the dross can be read and it offers to the individual insights into his biography that make it possible for him to live less unhappily. (Freud advances a good claim to be scientific: his hermeneutic of dreams is not another sort of art of reading tea leaves). Primitives value dreams much more highly: ancestors or gods continue the work of creation through the dreaming individuals. As G. Devereux puts if (of the Mohaves); "they interpret their culture by means of dreams, not their dreams in terms of their culture."[17] It is true that the Romantics tried to rehabilitate the value of dreams for Europeans. They saw in them bases for a resistance against what modern life was turning individuals into, namely cogs in some sort of machine, but they saw in them more an escape from society than a re-creation of it.

Dreams, concludes Bastide, are at the point of overlap between nature and culture. While the primitives see in them nature (that which is) coming to re-order culture (that which is customary), moderns tend to locate them in pure subjectivity and see in them confirmation of their ways and attitudes toward reason and efficiency. It is our ethnocentric culture that guides our interpretation of the mix of "natural" physiological and of "cultural" psychological phenomena that our science constructed. This is the occasion for him to make an important theoretical point. If we genuinely want a theory that applies to all cultures, we must characterize dreams in a broad enough way, which can be an umbrella for all kinds of dreams, and not be dogmatic about the relationship between nature and culture

Sociology and Psychology

In 1960 Bastide reviewed his life-long commitment to working out the relationship between sociology and psychology and wrote an article clarifying the history of this issue. He begins by noting that the discussion was made impossible by the focussing on two insoluble problems. First, many wasted their time trying to settle what comes first: society or the individual, a problem that can be solved only dogmatically. Then debates were clouded by "scientific" rivalry between the two disciplines: which one best explains human behaviour? In France Marcel Mauss gave in 1924 the terms for a truce by calling for the study of concrete cases. In their actions and interactions humans are always wholes, encompassing body, mental and social activity. To look at the total man, one needs co-operation between sociology and psychology. Gurvitch agreed and drew two overlapping circles to view the relationship between the two sciences. Lévi-Strauss affirmed that every social fact is also a mental fact. Therefore the tendency of some psychologists to overlook the cultural location of individuals as they study their responses to stimuli must be checked; sociologists also have their blind spots.

Bastide notes that in stable cultures social patterns are most accessible and psychological realities less visible. So the inquiry must find ways to move from the outside to the inside. In cultures that are being upset, and forced to effect a transition, the opposite is true: psychological realities are more accessible and social ones more fluid and elusive.

in a Western ethnocentric manner. (The same point can be made about theories of religion). We should not claim to know in advance what may result from what he called diving into darkness (*la plongée ténébreuse*). Our "scientific" views of dreams are not erroneous, but only partial. Our views in this area are again too often Promethean; they are constructed out of a dominant myth of human sovereign control.

The articles on trance give him an opportunity to recall his early distancing from Durkheim's view that religion arises out of wild outbursts and contagious emotional epidemics. For one thing, he discerned in what Durkheim himself was describing that the "breaking loose" was in fact ordered. Reading Mauss confirmed him in this opinion. The old fondness for the exotic and the barbaric is expelled from serious ethnographic studies. In the distant cults, we do not meet "original man" but other civilized human beings. Their trances are socialized, because they are potentially dangerous and because they, by themselves, bring no message.[18] So the trance is always domesticated. Africans and Afro-Brazilians make a distinction between normal, divine possession, which aggrandizes the individuals, and pathological possessions that torture them. In a public speech Bastide invites co-operation between ethnologists and psychiatrists. Possession is used to heal. He himself can attest that mental afflictions increased in Brazil in those cases when the police persecute the cults. Another conference calls attention to the difference between possession and shamanistic trance. Spirits remain exterior to the shaman; he dialogues or struggles with them. Possessions penetrate the core of the person.

Much then remains to be done, in his view, in the history of cults that feature possession. Typologies should be established. In the contemporary period, many of these change from cults of attestation and confirmation to cults of contestation.

One final article explores the complex relationship between the rituals of possession and the theatre. Historians argue that the theatre issued from ritualized trances, and avant-garde forms of theatre explore savage features. Some authors (Michel Leiris for Africa and Alfred Métraux for Haiti) have reported that rituals have begun to be shown as spectacles. Still, Bastide thinks that the rapprochement with avant-garde theatre is misleading. The African trance is a language, while the avant-garde theatre is a refusal of language; in this latter case the rejection of the social leads the self only to a more profound alienation in its own complexes.[19]

It was the problems arising from the encounter of civilizations that made Bastide interested in psychiatry. Cultures are standardized defensive systems and, in some historical circumstances of confrontation with or occupation by a foreign power, they fail to serve individuals well.[20] Social science weaves links between depth psychology and the "sociology of caves," namely the sociology that ventures into the darker areas of human interaction. Madness is not a fact but a problem; it comes only in shapes conditioned by the surrounding society. And shapes are individualized. There is no mental disease, only mental patients. (Sociology cannot dictate to psychology). Here again Bastide's sociology proves ambitious and holds the promise of making sense of the most unusual phenomena.

Beside the indication that mental afflictions increase when cults disintegrate, the set of articles on mental disease puts forward a definition of religion. "It takes its origin in a dissymmetry between polar categories: sacred and profane, high and low, right and left, initiate and non initiate, masculine and feminine, divine and demonic."[21] Since one pole is seen as positive and the other negative, great anxiety is produced by this dissymmetry in the individual. The religious world is constructed to restore symmetry between what is dissymmetrical, through myths and rites.[22] The definition is terse and somewhat cryptic. We will return to it and merely note now that it makes of religion a secondary affair, which copes with pre-existing cognitive stresses.

We can add one other lack of symmetry to the list indicated by Bastide: that between body and soul (or mind). The "place" mentioned in Charles Long's definition of religion, the place in which a human lives, is also, and perhaps primarily, his or her own body. Rachel E. Harding published her research on the condition in the nineteenth century of the Afro-Brazilians in the Northeast (based on police and court records). *Refuge in Thunder: Candomblé and Alternative Spaces of Blackness* does an excellent job of showing why corporeality should be shown as central to slave experience. (The point of course was already made in Gilberto Freyre's book). There is a very far-reaching sense in which the slaves' bodies are not their own. The colour of their skins is basis for the drawing of lines. (The lines are variable, but there are lines). They are manacled and fettered. The body is very much a contested site. When the gods ride the initiates, they reclaim their bodies. In trance and in dance, Afro-Brazilians re-capture their bodies. (The dance is a "symbolic re-elaboration of space"). She concludes that "the body as territory is at the heart of re-territorialization."[23] The history of Afro-Brazilian religion shows that the body is the place where freedom begins (or is reborn). Bastide does not put things so clearly but from his first text after his visit to the Northeast, where he saw bodies in motions new to him, to his last discussion of acculturation and mental distress, embodiment is constantly assumed to be the substratum to the life of the mind and the source of its fragility. Rachel Harding also suggests that it is the site of its victories.

The collection *Poètes et dieux. Études afro-brésiliennes* contains a 1953 article *Quelques considérations autour d'un "lavage de perle"* which deserves the attention of students of religion on three grounds.

First this description and study of the washing of the pearls which forms an important part of the initiation ritual for every prospective member of a *Candomblé* is for Bastide the occasion to establish his way of contrasting religion and magic. The future initiate must first consult the *babalao* to find out which god is going to be his master. This will determine what colour of beads he will henceforth wear as a necklace. The necklace will spend a whole night on the stone of the appropriate god. It will then be immersed in a pan of water. Herbs (of the appropriate kind and properly gathered) will be mashed and added to the water. (The blood of a hen may also be added). The water of the pan will then be used to wash either the head or the entire body of the initiate. Finally the necklace will be washed with sailors' soap (dark and soft, the kind used in Africa), and given to the initiate with instruction as to his new duties. The necklace is thus said to have been "baptized." Bastide argues that Frazer's law of magic, transfer of force through automatic contact, does not apply here. The whole process depends on many human interventions. First the judgement of the *babalao* is essential; he may make a mistake in the identification of the appropriate god; this sometimes happens and the wearer of the necklace ordinarily gets sick. Then the initiate must live up to his calling and not fail in his duties. There is no simple fluid-like transfer of *mana* when the pearls are on the stone or around the neck. Mystical participation does not occur in any and all directions. It must be oriented by human action, follow certain lines which depend on human involvement and choices, on moral and social realities. The scholar who summarizes his account with the statement: "they believe in magic—we don't," prevents the unveiling of a truth: all humans construct meaning through ritual action. The currencies that circulate among them include the (false?) currency of their dreams. And these enable them to frame expectations for the future.[24]

Second, the ritual implies a certain idea of participation. It assumes that there are intermediate positions between being and nothingness (as did medieval European ontologies). Wearing their necklace they participate in the divine reality AND in the social reality of their new religious community. When incorporated in Candomblé, the initiates move to a superior level of existence and acquire new ethical obligations. The idea of participation at work here is not just a feature of the primitive mentality outlined by Lévy-Brühl but a genuine philosophy of the cosmos available to all.

Thirdly the description is based on the washing of pearls done for Roger Bastide himself during his initiation in the night of August 3 and 4, 1951.

This will make his interpretation of the rite suspect to some. He of course saw everything close-hand; but it will also be said that he *believed* in it, and was not a mere participant-observer. In other words, on that night, he *did* religion and did not simply *study* it. That he defines this activity as religious rather than magical and makes of this analysis a cornerstone in his definition of religion only indicates, some will claim, a tainted subjective choice on his part, pushing participant observation a bit too far. On the other hand, one might advance that the quality of his description and analysis is a gain for all scholarship, no matter what tribute he personally paid. (A tribute, incidentally, which did not prevent his being buried in Anduze [Gard] according to the ritual of the Reformed Church). The point of this article, it seems to me, is to summon sociologists of religion examining the washing of pearls not to be satisfied with the conceptual work done by eighteenth century learned esoteric magicians who formulated theories of fluids, and transfer by contact. Sociology must also be attentive to the freely resolved actions of persons in the accounts it gives of rituals, or should abstain from speculating about what is going on and the meaning of it all. The pearls laid on the stone are an appeal; they are there because an individual supported by a community is turning to a god and calling on it.

If the three books on Afro-Brazilian cults are the solid pieces of scholarship one expects of university scholars, the collected articles gathered in the books of 1970–1973 are demonstrations of the fragility of the knowledge embodied selves rise to. Knowing subjects never develop their knowledge simply from the soil under their feet, the blood in their veins or the waves in their brains. (Myths abound to speak of the exceptional value of the soil, the blood or the waves). As separate subjects, knowing subjects stand inside limits of space and time, which separate them from other knowing subjects. To think well they need to cope with, or overcome, some limitations inherent in their situation. And the world of "other knowing subjects" is a very wide and varied one. While bodies can warm up or remain cold in contact with each other, bodies never speak—or, if they do, they speak metaphorically in the obscure language of desire or aversion, of posture and movements, of dreams, trances or pathological behaviour.

Bastide's chair in Paris was in ethnology. As an ethnologist he shared in the excitement and work of a generation of disenchanted and intellectually eager Europeans who roamed deep and wide in the worlds of foreign material and intellectual culture. They lived somewhat dangerously (at least intellectually dangerously) as they acknowledged the merits of intellectual confusion, and as they crossed wide chasms and gazed into bottomless pits. They physically involved themselves and contributed to a vast accumulation of data and to careful, self-critical accounts of foreign mentalities. As Bastide left the safe grounds of France and acculturated to Brazil, he left behind a world of clear definitions. In time, the near became far and the far near, reason became folly and folly reason. He enjoyed the lines in the contemporary song contrasting the ways of the US with those of Brazil.

> White is White, black is black, and *mulata* there is no such thing. Gay is gay, macho is macho, woman is woman, and money is money. That's how rights are bargained for, granted, won and lost up there. Down here, indefinition is the rule, and we dance with a grace that I myself can't explain.[25]

It is thanks to the science of sociology (as Bastide understood and developed it), that he worked his way up to consideration of general theoretical issues and, I might add, philosophical understanding.[26] The philosopher in us should be glad to know that around 1940, Wittgenstein, an Austrian then living in Cambridge, resolved to a huge effort: to defeat the bewitching effect language has on human minds. He undertook a systematic linguistic uprooting in himself, to view concepts in a new way, thereby opening the second period in his authorship. He did this at the time when French ethnologists like Bastide were busy de-culturating and re-acculturating themselves. And this led to the *Philosophical Investigations* published in 1953, a book which contains a revealing comparison: "When we do philosophy we are like savages, primitive people, who hear the expressions of civilised men, put a false interpretation on them and then draw the queerest conclusions from it."[27]

Chapter 8

Candomblé as paradigm for translocal religion

Religion is for many people still a territorialized reality. This is reflected in dictionary definitions and stems from years of construction of religion by Western theologians, philosophers and historians. The Crusades ended with the drawing up of a strong line between Muslim and Christian lands. The sixteenth century reforms carved out Europe into Catholic and Protestant countries. Twentieth century Jews struggled to create and defend a Jewish land. Bastide's work focussed on one of the contemporary religions in which the urge to achieve hegemony over a territory is weak or absent. As he explored various facets of the life and history of Candomblé, he was led into numerous thematic and methodological revolutions. Bastide's work forces itself on the attention of scholars of religion for two reasons. He sketched a general picture of all Afro-American cults (in both Americas). He showed that what Candomblé exhibits is not more of the same kind of religion, because it is an instance of an alternative metaphysics, another way of carving out reality.[1]

Fernando Giobellina Brumana wrote that the focus on Afro-Brasilian cults is a gift of French scholars.[2] Bastide forced serious attention upon it and wrote what became the classical corpus. He clearly broke with the trend that studied Afro-Brazilians in order to exercise power over them (power intended to be beneficent to be sure, to bring them into the mainstream). Verger brought further depth to his study with his photographic art and with a reorienting of the geographic imagination and with documentation on the trans-Atlantic traffic. The slaves were transported from Nigeria to Pernambuco and Bahia, the place where the Atlantic is at its narrowest.[3] It was her training in Paris that led the Argentinian Juana Elbein dos Santos to do the monumental study on death in Bahia.[4]

Candomblé thus became an early and major exhibit of a religion born of acculturation, of the meeting between two civilizations. It became a lab in which crucial notions were elaborated. Memory is not just storage but selection of what is meaningful under the circumstances. It includes bodily practices. In areas of cultural contact, societies are constituted by an overlap of multiple imagined communities. All classes have an interest in projecting their imagination but some are more empowered to project it. So the scholar finds a number of interpretative frames that require nothing but imagination to make them real, and a number of groups that compete for possession of signs.

"Stagism," namely the construction of a progressive sequence in world history is a complete obfuscation of the facts. It reflects the belief of the enlightened scholars that they, and they alone, see and understand all cultures, while others remain insulated in their local and narrow outlook. The notion of "roots" must be discarded, and also that of "survivals", conceived as features of an earlier stage in the evolutionary ladder that outlast the days when they served a purpose. Synchronic events must be described in terms of borders (shifting, of course) and of liminality, in terms of phenomena of inclusion and exclusion. Diachronic events must be understood in terms of resistance, hybridation, and transmission of memory and forgetting. The scholar should never underestimate the capacity of the individual to imagine belonging in multiple communities and to shift the locales of his belonging. And neither should he overlook the fact that interrelationship and interaction take place even when the partners are not on an even playing field. What Freyre taught Bastide on the sexual and family mores of the plantation seems to me to have been a decisive nudge that forced an inquiry into all aspects of liminality and symbolic exchanges in daily life. And these exchanges are thick-layered. It is not true that the only alternative is between obedience and revolt. Lots of people comply but do not submit. There can be both oppression and a measure of reciprocity. (Is reciprocity ever perfect?) Any lived religion therefore must be viewed, like power relations, within the richest possible account of the social context.[5]

Bastide's attention to the phenomena of participation makes clear what is at stake in the claim about an alternative metaphysic. People cannot be both Portuguese and African, so they became Brazilian. What happened however should not be compared to what results from pouring black dye into a can of white paint. (Genetics encouraged such views). Western thought (since Aristotle) and Western religion (since the definition of Christian orthodoxy) have operated on the law of the excluded middle. One cannot both be enlightened and religious, both Christian and Jewish, or both cosmopolitan and ethnic. But Candomblé shows a constant recourse to the law of the included middle. Hybridation (or *mestiçagem* to use the Portuguese term) is not the production of a stable mix or blend. It is a continuous process.[6] There is juxtaposition, overlapping, shifting emphases, temporary watertight compartments. Against some commonly held views of syncretism, people are quite capable of adhering simultaneously to diverse, heterogeneous beliefs. It is true that Candomblé recreates something of Africa. The large public hall where the daughters and sons of the gods dance is a reproduction of the village square. But the *terreiro* is not the sort of transplanted African village that Disneyworld offers. Ogun is both an *orixa*, a god, and a Christian saint. But people are not fooled. He is more one in some contexts, and more the other in others. If religion for Bastide overcomes dissymmetry, it does not do away with the polarity. In Hegelian terms, we would have to say that the synthesis does not take up all that is valuable in the thesis and the antithesis; residues remain.

This is what I mean when I argue that Bastide "invented" Candomblé. He put it on the map for all to see. Candomblé achieved a new substantiality through recognition. When Simone de Beauvoir travelled in America she stopped in Bahia, met with priestesses, and with Pierre Verger, Gilberto Freyre and Jorge Amado, and thought it over. She wrote 14 pages in *La Force des choses* where she sees this religion as a noble form of resistance.[7]

Candomblé became a religion among others, like the others in some ways, but original in others. Matory's book, *Black Atlantic religion*, illustrates and fully documents the process that ensued from what was started in the late 1940s. First, the Brazilian oscillation between persecution and protection of Afro-Brazilian cults clearly stopped in the 1980s.[8] Candomblé has joined the list of "official" or recognized cults and enjoys the freedom of religion the Constitution affirms. It has become part of *patrimonio*; this means that some of its historical sites have been maintained with public heritage funds that were created to restore colonial palaces and baroque churches. The drive to Africanize it during the 1980s, with the moves to remove traces of Catholicism from the *terreiros*, helped make it look like a self-sufficient religion. The affirmation of religious freedom by the Second Vatican Council in the 1960s helped the Catholic Church see Candomblé as an external colleague rather an internal threat.

Secondly, dialogue and co-operation got going among the cults. Gilberto Freyre organized the first Afro-Brazilian Congress as early as 1934. Since 1937 the Union of Afro-Brazilian Sects works to regulate priestly conduct and oppose police repression. The movement became international. The University of Ifè (Nigeria) hosted the World Conference of Orisha Tradition and Culture in 1981.

Thirdly, a spate of competent authors, including US ones, studied Candomblé and published major specialized works on aspects of it. We already referred to the book of G. Rachel Harding. The ecological wave praised the religion for its closeness to nature. The idiom of purity (African purity) caused another wave. Ruth Landes was much read in the US with her book, *The City of Women,* which documents the increasing power of the mothers of saints (or shift in the leadership) and promoted feminist views. Candomblé is said to be matriarchal, and a resource for the destruction of Western sources of sexism.[9] Robert A. Voeks gave a study with strong ethno-botanic content: *Sacred Leaves of Candomblé. African Magic, Medicine and Religion in Brazil.*[10] Paul Christopher Johnson contributed *Secrets, Gossip and Gods: The Transformation of Brazilian Candomblé*. Starting with participant observation in a small (and impoverished) *terreiro* in Rio de Janeiro he expanded his work on the study of historical layers of secrecy and showed how Candomblé now prospers by revealing its secrets.[11] And Floyd Merrell offered an illuminating study drawing parallels between the religion and the sport-dance-martial art that developed among Afro-Brazilians: *Capoeira and Candomblé: Conformity and Resistance in Brazil.*[12]

Finally, scholars who study the religion and devotees who do it started meeting each other at conferences. Matory discusses at some length the events that occurred during the 1999 conference held at Florida International University. Under the title "Orisa Devotion as a World Religion: The Globalization of Yoruba Religious Culture," the meeting was attended by US based scholars of various backgrounds, along with Trinidadians and Brazilian scholars with links to Nigeria, Cuba and Puerto-Rico. Various priestesses and priests were also present. Matory comments on the nostalgia, imaginings and silencing exhibited in these gatherings. The conference brought further proof that life imitates scholarship.[13] This fact was already illustrated when Bastide's doctoral thesis was used to establish views about genuine Candomblé. Clearly Candomblé is now well launched on the career of what might be called a major minor international religion; it shows all its strains and stresses. And in Brazil, it functions, as Johnson puts it, like a sort of "Protestant denomination."

Matory's overall argument is about trans-local and trans-national religion, for which Candomblé serves as an excellent paradigm. The habit of territorialization blinded scholars to trade routes (on land and sea) and to the inter-relatedness and interaction of religions on such routes.[14] Many scholars focus their attention now on what is called "contact places". Diaspora studies are in full bloom among Hindus and Jews. Matory suggests that Candomblé studies, which energized and enriched studies on US Afro-American religion, could also bring tested tools to these other emerging studies. The notion of globalization, I might add, should not become the exclusive possession of neo-liberal economics.

Chapter 9

O Sacrado Selvagem as corner stone of a theory of religion

The distinction between *the sacred* and *the profane* is taught in most introductory courses in sociology of religion, with obligatory reference to the work of Durkheim. The distinction brings about a bipartite division of the entire universe. Sacred things are protected and isolated by interdictions; profane things are under rules emanating from these interdictions.[1] A definition of religion follows: "A religion is a unified system of beliefs and practices relative to sacred things."[2]

In Durkheim's works the sacred looks very much like a wafer ensconced in a precious container (hidden in a tabernacle, with its presence signalled by a little flame giving a small red light), or like a scroll wrapped in embroidered velvet and with a gold crown on top. In fact *res sacrae* (cultic utensils) is the oldest appearance of the term. The behaviour of believers in front of sacred objects tends to become objectified. (Durkheim made it a rule to treat social facts as things). To Bastide, these visions of cult objects direct the thinking about religion into the wrong directions. Durkheim's definition does not work well with Low Church Protestantism, which has no strict ritual rules on how to handle the Bible or how to use the space in a church building. Bastide would also doubt that religions are "systems" that are as unified as Durkheim says.

Many authors coming after Durkheim reworked the notion of the sacred in their own ongoing search for the distinctive character of religion. In 1917, coming from a very different world, Rudolf Otto, a German protestant theologian who knew of great deal more history of religions than Durkheim, seized upon another Latin word and introduced the notion of the numinous. *The Idea of the Holy*[3] gives a more theistic focus to his inquiry (*numen* means deity) and leads to a theory of the individual feeling from which religion allegedly takes its rise. He was much influenced by Schleiermacher, the nineteenth century German theologian, who defined religion as feeling. Otto's work is significant also in that it stresses the ambivalent characteristic of the numinous: it is a *mysterium tremendum.* The numinous both draws and repels; it fascinates and frightens.[4]

In 1939 Roger Caillois unfolded his notion of the sacred in *Man and the Sacred.*[5] He also stressed the ambiguity between positive and negative aspects of the sacred, but his look went much beyond the boundaries of religions. He was part of a group of younger intellectuals, including Georges Bataille and Michel Leiris, who were reading Marcel Mauss, and tried to understand the deep springs of collective existence. Their readings in ethnology were abundant and they hoped to derive from this new science tools to understand the human predicament in the Europe of the thirties. They worked together in their own *Collège de sociologie.*[6] They were all much preoccupied by the appeal that Nazism and communism had on "modern" minds, who were no longer in the grip of tradition, and by the blandness of the intellectual response democracies could muster. With them, the sacred is clearly differentiated between the sacred of respect, source of social norms, and the sacred of transgression, manifested in the feast. Ultimately the sacred is ambivalent: it is source of order and of disorder, and is therefore both a condition of life and a dangerous door leading to death. It both regulates culture and finds a way to exit from culture. Appendices illustrate the diffuse nature of the sacred by discussing sex, play and war, as contexts in which the ordinary borders set to behaviour are suspended. These French authors are of course much more attentive to wild and very physical group behaviour than Otto ever was. With the German theologian the notion of God as stern moral judge found in the Bible sufficed to illustrate the negative side of the numinous. (God could indeed be very angry). In sharp contrast, George Bataille delved with deep fascination into religious forms of extreme pain, into cases of bloody sacrifice, passionate transgression, wild surrender and ecstasies that suspend or annihilate the life of the self. He analyses feasts as orgies of expense, bringing about destruction of wealth and erasure of individual consciousness. Extreme pain joins extreme pleasure in the frenzied disappearance of the separate self into undifferentiated whole. The worlds of sex, pain and death thus become joined in a sort of celebration of the capturing power of the sacred. Bataille is the strongest antidote to the Durkheimian view of societies always striving to achieve a state of homeostasis. Humans do cause chaos. But, influenced as he was by Nietzsche, his general view of transgression tended to overlook the difference between sending Louis XVI to the guillotine and decapitating the statues of the kings in the façade of Notre-Dame. Bataille's contribution to scholarship should be considered thin, but he shaped sensibilities and had a powerful literary impact.[7]

In 1959 Mircea Eliade published *The Sacred and the Profane: The Nature of Religion*. The book profited from the vast erudition of the author and gained wide currency.[8] The author begins by stressing the influence of Otto (an omnipresent influence among German and English-speaking historians of religion of his generation) and the human inability to express the "totally other." In Eliade's view, the sacred manifests itself as "wholly different" from the profane in two different modes, as sacred space and sacred time. Eliade writes of hierophanies, manifestations of the sacred, and thus makes the sacred/profane distinction a basic ontological datum. The contrast then is sketched between those who live in a sacralized stable cosmos where time sequences are orderly, and those in modern societies who live in discontinuous historical time and a desacralized cosmos.

A respected French historian, Alphonse Dupront wrote a weighty cultural history of French Christianity under the title *Du Sacré* (1987). The book offers itself as an exploration into the mental depths of Western (Catholic) humans. Through studies of the crusades and pilgrimages, the book focuses on the power exhibited by "the sacred," when it grasps believers and informs their action. The sacred in this case is manifested in the continuities of culture, in the mentalities attested in a long period of time (*longue durée).* This notion is still in use among historians.[9]

Whether in Europe or in America this sequence of major works kept the idea of the sacred in currency and helped paint the processes of modernization with a very broad brush (a tendency, incidentally, that is of very little help to historians of early modern Europe). In the case of Eliade, it also led to a spiritual outlook based on belief in the enduring significance of the sacred. None of it seems to have had much impact on Bastide. This ethnologist was too attentive to diversity to be interested in those trying to find the core of religion (or of modernity), or the essence of either.

It is noteworthy that the concept of the sacred makes only scant appearances in the work of Bastide. Clearly he did not find the concept to be a convenient tool. When he finally did use to good effect, he appended the epithet "savage" and thus linked the experience of the sacred to chaotic contexts of disintegration and rebirth of integration. This should not surprise us, as he assimilated a version of Christian theology that focussed more on prophecy than on priesthood.

Commenting on a well-known page from the Bible may help understand what Bastide is talking about in this final statement. The sacred may well be the locale where God is about to appear, but Exodus 19, describing what happened at Sinai, is quite clear: the people are not allowed to set foot on the shaking mountain that is surrounded by lightning and smoke. And the people don't seem to want to. Sacred and profane in this case are not primarily mental categories that serve to map out the world. They are the source of deep affective and physical reactions. (Paul joins fear with trembling). They are also the occasion of a command. Whether thundering, luminous mountain, or dark, silent, gaping hole, the sacred is what Everyman is told to stay away from. Ordinarily Everyman wants to keep a distance, because he wants meaning and order above all, and finds both thanks to fellowship and reassurance in shared language and shared ritual. The sacred is neither malevolent nor benevolent; it is simply unbearable. It is a relief for humans when they get The Law, transmitted when Moses came down, because it orders their lives. In other words, it maps out in practical terms the undescribable impact of the secret encounter of the prophet-legislator with God.[10] The sacred is the ultimate boundary, the one humans most dread. It is the one religion protects us from, to some extent. The savage sacred then is the area of proximity between what is beyond the boundary and what gets organized at a distance from it. It is the area of maximal cognitive stress.

There is now one word that can be used to "reveal" the secret lying beyond the boundary: death. It is death, the line that one crosses only once, that causes the terror, and forces the improvisation of a response.[11] The invented response may be frantic, disorganized at first, in one word *savage*. But societies develop in time some more stable, ritualized responses, brought to some intellectual clarity thanks to a mythology of some sort. This institutionalization is what may properly be called religion.

The savage sacred therefore is a creation, not a repetition. As creation it is linked to *anomie*, namely the absence of law. Durkheim coined the term in his study *Suicide* (1897) and saw in the phenomenon the major cause of suicide. But he left it at that; his subsequent work focused on the construction of order and neglected the closer look at what he would have called social pathologies. What we get from Bastide is the insight that the manifestations of the savage sacred are moments of anomie that put up a barrier to worse forms of anomie. In other words, anomie comes in various shades. And many forms of anomie are not violent. The confusion between savagery and violence, common in the colonial era, is blind to facts.[12]

Bastide does not find much that is sacred in organized religion and its props. He is more interested in those places and moments when religion is being born, starting to enhance life, in contact with the savage sacred but promptly at some remove from it.[13] On his view, humans ordinarily do not want to slide into death and the ensuing absence from daily life and concerns, but prefer remaining living in their bodies and in touch with each other. The extinction of our time-bound and space-bound existence should not be construed as a merging with "reality" (even if qualified as ultimate). This "reality" bears no resemblance with what we ordinarily mean by that. Language places us on civilized grounds that are different from those mute and raw extreme experiences, which bring our separate selves in proximity with extinction. Bastide here keeps using the contrast between the present (and active) participle and the past (immobile) participle that had been used to great effect by Spinoza and by Bergson. Language, being instituted, can attest only to that which is instituted, but can also suggest the line beyond which lies the instituting. Language enables us to pursue the work of living together.[14] In a similar way rationality cannot organize the irrational messes over against which it defines and establishes itself. Praxis cannot ignore or seal off the forces of chaos, but it contends against them. As his difference from Lévi-Strauss well shows, the study of religion for Bastide is not the study of myths as depositories of mental operations. The study of religion does not focus on what all humans always do, but on what some humans in some group actually do to stay alive.[15] Intelligence is at work in religion but it is embedded in praxis, because humans who do religion are always caught between memory and anticipation, two aspects of mental life humans cannot entirely abstract themselves from since they are intimately related to their consciousness of their time-bound condition.

I might say therefore that, as a scholar, Bastide wanted to study the way spiders build their webs, and see what the webs look like and how they change, rather than establishing the spot where spiders tie their work to some exterior stable point. In a similar vein, Desroche evoked the fakir who throws his rope in the air. This sociologist directed our imaginations to the mysterious moment when the rope raises straight up and becomes solid, so that the fakir or his assistant can climb up, as if the rope was hooked to some invisible point above.[16] One can also make the point by stating that for Bastide, as for Gurvitch, symbols are signs, that are substitutes that cope with an absence.[17] In no sense are they the presence of what they symbolize. (The distinction echoes the terms of the Eucharistic controversy that raged in the sixteenth century: is the bread the body of Christ or the symbol of it?)

The web of religion might then be visualized as a series of concentric circles around the mountain or hole, circles which spread, through many intermediate grounds, all the way to a horizon, which would be a purely profane plain. This purely profane environment is best found in the worlds described by literary dystopias, the deserts where language is dead, poetry impossible, and where there is no duty to be, no virtualities to be realized in the future. (Visualize a dead planet, where everything that is the case can be put in mathematical formulas). Bastide's account of the trance in Candomblé, like that of the great Christian mystics, is that these religious persons can come to the edge of the mountain or hole, but if they are still here to tell us about it, they neither climbed nor fell. So the study of religion is the study of humans looking for signs and using signs in the long middle ground between the dark abyss and the sterile plains of insignificant measurements.

This metaphor of the edge of the precipice appears at least three times in his work. In his article on US cultural anthropologists, Bastide states that they are seduced by the appeal from primitive societies but build a fence to prevent themselves from falling, and produce a succession of theories to stop them from falling.[18] In private notes brooding over the festive turmoil caused in French universities by the disturbances of May 1968, he writes he is both seduced by the drunken exaltation and intensely curious about the destructuration and restructuration that is going on. He adds that, likes Ulysses, he ties himself to the mast, because he wants to hear the sirens, not drown in the midst of their song.[19] Claude Ravelet quotes a paper found posthumously on the "pit of the sacred": "I am told that I love it, as long as there is a railing."[20] It is in such a context that I propose to interpret his statement that "all our religions are secularized."[21] What the scholar in him calls religion is always to be contextualized, embodied in language: it is done in history, in localized and dated circumstances. And history is secular; it occurs in the *saeculum*.

"Shaking mountain" and "dark abyss" are metaphors to point to a fount (another metaphor) of disorder, that more or less unpredictably forces destructuring and restructuring of all orders. Henri Desroche, Bastide's friend and colleague, documented the historical persistence of these forces in the marginal forms of Western religious consciousness, the numerous sectarian movements that erupted in times of crisis, and upset some firmly drawn lines—and which he called "religions of contraband."[22] Contraband is an apt metaphor for all the traffic of ideas and symbols across established borders, which unfailingly cause tremors and disturb or disrupt the social system. Bastide and Desroche encouraged the study of religious institutions that achieve and launch innovative action, of the cases where the imagination brings about change. The dominant practices of power limit the possibilities inherent in the culture of any group.[23] But the pots of memory can be stirred up, as they were by Afro-Brazilians. What Mauss and Bastide called *attente* and can be translated as expectation is a most potent stirring power,[24] as is manifest in messianic movements.

Clearly in the case of Bastide the urge to be a sober scholar (and law-abiding citizen) prevailed over the eros for ecstatic experiencing, and provocative scandal.[25] He knows he is, like everyone else, an embodied person who needs a backbone to keep his body from falling, and a society with working norms to give him company and protection. Those who get burned on the mountain or drowned in the hole cease to be because they no longer have bodies and friends. To be alive is to be inseparably embodied, social and able to use the tools of language.[26] At no point does Bastide toy with the idea that humans might make it without language or should resist its pre-eminence in common life, since it is our best tool for maintaining civility and justice. When Baudelaire invited his readers to experience drunkenness, he listed three options: to be drunk on wine, on poetry or on virtue.[27] Bastide chooses the second option. To him there is no ethic of salvation without an ethic of moral order and poetry is an adjuvant to that.[28]

But we know there is no order without disorder—or the threat of it, just as there is no justice without the threat of injustice. Ethics inevitably involves delving into interactions, passions and messy affective realities that are not likely to be settled once and for all by clear and carefully enforced norms. All study in the humanities is necessarily nourished by the study of inhumanity. This focus is already illustrated in the *Epic of Gilgamesh* and the *Iliad.*

Bastide's extreme sensitivity to the presence of potential conflict in social interaction and to the moral work done daily by language and institutions led him to write an article on a controversy that had arisen in 1965 between Maurice Leenhardt and Claude Lévi-Strauss.[29]

Bastide found in the Leenhardt—Lévi-Strauss contrast an echo of the older divergence between Durkheim and Lucien Lévy-Brühl. Like the former, Lévi-Strauss believes in the unity of reason; as a scholar he attempts explanations. Like Lévy-Brühl, Leenhardt sees the multiplicity of reasons and he begins by attempting to understand. The first, like Descartes, wants to rise about the level of bodily-induced confused thoughts, to arrive at the world of forms. The second points out that what is empirically given is society, which can be inventoried and described, but cannot be scientifically analysed since tools of analysis come from the minds that were trained in different cultures and employ historically constructed tools of analysis. Leenhardt therefore came to the conclusion that what he found among the Canaques was another form of knowledge, not an inferior one. Our analytical thinking cuts up what they, with their mental categories, see united. They participate in both what we call separate A and B. With them, the border between the different and the identical is fuzzy—and the selves are not cut off from the world. In other words Canaques are nearer the area of proximity from the savage sacred while Western rationalists are

Maurice Leenhardt (1876–1954)

The paths followed by Leenhardt and the younger Bastide did not meet but a convergence between their intellectual interests and careers should be noted. Leenhardt arrived in New Caledonia in 1902 as protestant missionary and pursued his ministry as he studied the languages, customs and myths of this group of Melanesian peoples. Before Malinowski ever arrived in the Trobriand Islands (1915, for three years), Leenhardt elaborated the technique of participant observation, the fruits of which became manifest in his book *Do Kamo* (1947, English 1972). This ethnographer gives a positive value to his affective involvement with the life of the New Caledonians. The reality of participation between self and other is not labelled as the keynote of a "primitive" mentality and magic, but viewed as a reality of all human living.

Leenhardt translated the New Testament and the Psalms into houaïlou, with great care in the establishment of appropriate terminology. He returned to Paris in 1926, to teach in a Mission school, and soon to become the assistant of Marcel Mauss and fellow teacher. In 1942, he succeeded Mauss in the chair at the École Pratique des Hautes Études. (He was succeeded in it by Claude Lévi-Strauss). His teaching position in Paris did not sever his bonds with New Caledonia; he returned to it in 1938–1940 and in 1947 founded and became director of the Institut Français d'Océanie.

He was a politically minded missionary and an activist ethnologist. When he arrived in New Caledonia, the French colonists had seized the land from the natives and tried to put them to work, but, unsatisfied with the results, had brought more cost-efficient Indonesians. They also brought convicts—who, when freed, got their income by selling liquor to the natives. Leenhardt got in conflict with the colonial authorities. His understanding of the mentality of the Canaques (divided into 36 dialects) gave him views and strategies to enhance their chances for life under the new conditions. Being self-critical, walking in the shoes of the natives, he could sense what they needed to promote their own existence and worked hard to support their efforts.

closer to the mathematised world where A is always A and only A.

Such awareness about the limitations of mental categories and such commitment to cultural pluralism force upon us the question of the kind of language that should be used by the scholar. We might be guided here by an aphorism of Oscar Wilde. *Truth pure and simple is rarely pure and never simple*. We shall focus on this issue in our last section. For now let us simply note that, beside the language issuing from human mouths, there is also the language of human bodies. Not much attention was paid to that in the churches Bastide attended in his childhood but he quickly got the point in the Brazilian Northeast. Furthermore live discourse, verbal and physical, happens between persons in relations. As Ricoeur put it many times, discourse is someone saying something about something to someone, using a shared code. Two points must be seen here. The persons spoken to are different from the speaker; discourse lives in a context of otherness. And the persons are alive; they move and change.

Bastide, we said, took the risk of acculturation. He did not travel for rest and recreation but for growth in knowledge and wisdom. All his ethnological work is concerned with identifying gaping spaces, wide or narrow distances, ditches and chasms. His work is thus always concerned with describing what happens to humans who stand on borders and come into one of the many possible forms of contact and exchange with the other. And realities, we must emphasize, are asymmetrical. Drawing lines should not lead to drawing reverse identical images on each side. The one who is facing the self is not a mirror image of the self.

Borders are of course self-protecting; but they are also places where one can look over the fence and see something different. There is an inherent promise about being on the frontier. Some borders become places of death, others are enlivening. What happens there is never easy to describe, since each side approaches the task of description with languages developed and stabilized in the territories behind the fence. Gilbert Durand mentions the poverty of the translation Bastide had to settle for when he put into French the title of Freyre's great work. *Casa grande e senzala* refers to the manorial house and the slave quarters. Brazilian readers know that traffic occurs between the two locations. *Maîtres et esclaves* directs the minds of French readers toward the opposition in status and thereby erects a wall.[30] Bastide knew he had to convert in some sense, to change his "scientific mentality" to write the history of Afro-Brazilian cults, and he said so.[31] Self-fecundation exists in botany, but it does not exist among humans. Bastide's life and scholarship is predicated on the assumption that self-fecundation is never an intellectual option.

If Bastide's whole work is dedicated to the blurring of the lines between "us and them," he does not erase them. Because people on either side of what began as a border move, and change according to their own logic and needs. Freedom is not abolished when people meet. One might even say that it starts in earnest at his point. "Syncretism" is a process that never ends; it is not the building of some new synthesis that causes differences to disappear. It bears no resemblance to the ideal religion that well-intentioned and peace-minded scholars tried to assemble for the benefit of all humankind, or of some part of it. A more apt illustration of syncretism is the case of the Maroons of Surinam who say their Catholic prayers while facing, Muslim style, the city of Cayenne.[32] Or the case of the Afro-Brazilians who returned to Africa and built in Dahomey mosques that look like baroque churches.

Bastide's way of mapping the terrain of cultural contact and acculturation owes much to what he learned from Gurvitch, more specifically from his "sociology of freedom"[33] and his way of moving back and forth between macro and micro sociology. Gurvitch urged his readers to pay attention to three types of social groupings constructed to help humans cope with the obstacles they encounter: masses, communities and communions. In masses the self has minimal participation in the group and the attraction of the self to it is also minimal. In communions, the attraction is at its maximum, and the felt pressure on the self is least; the relationship between the self and "Us" is close to fusion—and the group remains small to maintain the intensity of its common belonging. Communions stand halfway in all three dimensions of attraction, pressure and participation.[34] Ordinarily selves have links with all three kinds of groups. The truth about their social life therefore cannot a simple opposition between "me and them." To this analysis Gurvitch adds a notion of diversity of "social times," a diversity which causes relationships to be in modes of conflict or convergence (with many intermediate states).[35] All types of social relations are always dependent on the extent to which both sides are ready for them.

The influence of Gurvitch confirmed what Bastide could already learn from Mauss. Society is always in the making and remaking. Collective representations are set in motion by memory and by expectations. Cultural transmission is a live historical process. What has been made can be, and must be, remade. The French sociologists and anthropologists who shared this theory of society also had a (related) political agenda. Lack of purity is a source of strength.[36] Cultural homogeneity and ethnic purity provide only a weak form of energy. Prosperous trees do not derive their nourishment only from deep roots safely hidden in the soil but also from leaves exposed to the sun and the atmosphere—and to the accidents of the climate. The young Bastide was already on this wavelength when he warned his students that regional folklore is not what is kept in museums.

Chapter 10

Study of religion and sociology of knowledge

We said that the larger disciplinary framework within which Bastide theorises about religion is that of sociology. We can be more specific and define his contribution to a sociology of knowledge. While his interests were wide-ranging, including for instance ethno-psychiatry and processes of decolonization, we should situate the culminating point of his scholarly career in 1965 when he came to preside over the Sorbonne research group in sociology of knowledge. In this capacity, his path as a scholar was based on two premises.

1. The theorist cannot ever absolutely abstract his work from his own personal context. If he cuts his moorings from the society of his birth and youth, he gets acculturated into another. If he divorces himself from a religious tradition, he trails something of it behind himself. If he criticizes (or revolts against) a scholarly tradition, he embeds himself into another (which sometimes is only the opposite of the first). And when he writes with his best professional conscience, he has a language and hence a scholarly public. Furthermore, he has also a style. This is where his chance lies, as we shall see in the next section; because language can accommodate styles that do not make their own categories absolute but set the readers' minds in motion.

A masterful defence of this point is found in Pierre Bourdieu's *Pascalian Meditations.*[1] We are implicated in a world, from which we distance ourselves in our scholarly work. No human ever achieved a radical enough doubt to suspend all presuppositions. It is true that as schoolchildren and later as intellectuals in universities we have the time to cultivate the arts of reflexivity, detachment and methodical inquiry. Thus some come to believe they are scholars living above the urgencies of everyday life.[2] The philosopher, writes Bourdieu, "is like every one, comprehended in the space he seeks to comprehend." This sociologist asks therefore for a "differential anthropology of symbolic forms" and awareness of the varieties of cognitive dispositions.[3] I see Bastide building his scholarly work on the premise that all humans, as individuals and as groups, develop their own (and much diversified) forms of memory and anticipation. All his readers can see him acknowledging his intellectual sources.[4]

2. The theorist talks about all the forms of knowledge. They are diverse and in constant motion. His focussed statements catch one layer of knowledge at one time and in a limited area. Through amassing data and classifying them into ideal types, he can proceed with comparative work, and venture into generalizations and identification of tendencies. We stressed that Bastide was sympathetically attentive to what he saw Afro-Brazilians or Africans do, but his contribution is very different from what is ordinarily meant by the fruits of empathy in religious scholarship.[5] Beginning unashamedly with empathetic sympathy was not granting himself a free rein for the expression of his subjectivity. Because after empathy came the huge body of comparative ethnographic work and the general scientific theory of acculturation. And what came out from there was a wide-ranging critique of the intellectual tools commonly available then, coupled to an obstinate desire to construct better ones. Consider, for instance, the amount of deconstruction that had to be done of what was in previous times considered to be self-evident objects: magic, religion, race, fetishism, animism, totemism, primitive monotheism. There were days when Western scholars handled these topics as if they were insects pinned on their corks. It is the input from two generations of field ethnographers on at least two continents that makes his sociology of knowledge of contemporary interest.

We can add that learning from the ethnographers has a specific advantage for students of religion, which his generation of French scholars fully exploited. We saw that it involved a measure of uprooting and adventure and required a measure of acculturation. The point now is that this enables students of religion to go round what is still for many the vexing problem of belief. It is commonly said that all people have beliefs. That is true, as far as it goes. But some beliefs are more imperious than others. And most importantly, some are more visible than others. Why should a Christian be considered at the outset more biased, less fit to study religion, than a member of the Labour Party? The answer is quickly given: the West has since at least the eighteenth century been the stage of a uniquely powerful and strongly polarized movement opposing "Christian believers" to all other Western people. Furthermore, in the world of comparative scholarship, the attempt to define the religious beliefs of people on other continents has been the central inquiry in at least two centuries' worth of research into other cultures. (Theologians, historians of religion and early anthropologists all shared this curiosity for "beliefs," even when they shared little else, and pursued their heated intra-Western polemics). Scholars of various hues filled library shelves with studies ignoring the fact that language enters into experience itself.[6] As Rodney Needham pointed out, belief is an operation of the mind and the only evidence we have of it is the statement the "believer" makes. We should therefore consider belief to be a private state of mind that cannot be analysed.[7] It should be clear by now that beliefs, Christian or other, are hard to pin down (unless one consults the written official creeds) and unlikely to become objects of science. This is especially true now that customary religious beliefs that had once demonstrable impact on the majority have evaporated from the lives of many individuals in many societies. Inquiries into beliefs favoured by the social scientists of the 1970s turned out to be little else but opinion surveys. It became notoriously difficult to predict behaviour from beliefs professed by individuals.[8]

Why should scholarly suspicion then focus on scholars who acknowledge they have beliefs? The most serious problem is not that personal beliefs pollute some scholarship (which is sometimes undoubtedly the case), but that the cultural background of all inquirers limits—sometimes very severely—the range of the results they conscientiously put forward. In other words, the conditioning factors must be re-identified and the core importance previously accorded to religious beliefs should be replaced by broader histories of meaning and of ideologies. And this is done by sociology of knowledge, more specifically, a sociology of knowledge-in-action.

Awareness of the multiplicity of cultures present in an apparently unified society, coupled to the awareness that these cultures have both enabling and impairing cognitive consequences, enable us to do away with the simple generalizations about modernity that are sometimes taken for granted among theorists of religion. The construction of the modern West in its singularity is the outcome of many diverse processes of acculturation. First came that evolution of national kingdoms, most notoriously France and England, where kings managed to become sacralized, as was made manifest from their coronation ceremonies and even their abilities to make miracles. Then increasingly powerful royal law won battles against ecclesiastical law, and the Crowns could appropriate real estate owned by the Church. (This was called secularizing the lands). After the lawyers, and at first overlapping with them, came the humanists, who cultivated letters and criticism of documentary evidence. They also taught good writing and formal public speaking. They brought back the culture of antiquity into the arts and schools. Then came the educators, whose Latin-speaking male students became estranged from the women in their families and around them.[9] There came also the religious reformers (active in religious orders and in the Church, in the case of men and women, or based in universities in the case of males only) and finally the male artisans of the scientific revolution and the ideologies this gave rise to. This gives us a short list of six foci of diffusion of new cultural attitudes and habits—and I have not even mentioned the merchants and bankers who invented cheques. They were certainly not unanimous in their views of the desirable future or in their working for the promotion of "modernity."

Bastide's most condensed statement on the sociology of knowledge is found in a 1979 article "Mémoire collective et sociologie du bricolage."[10] He begins by summarizing the impact of Afro-American studies on wider fields of study: these studies showed the importance of "internal causality" (i.e. what people and groups chose to do) and led to an assessment of the reproductive and creative role of imagination in the lives of people. He then turns to a review of the contribution of Maurice Halbwachs; the alternative between physiology and sociology dictated by Durkheim is not valid. Consciences are permeable to each other. A social system does not function on the basis of communion but only through communication. There is also a constant interaction between bodies and space. Bodies too are bearers of myths. To last, religious groups need material support, objects and spaces. (The Church put Ways of the Cross in all its buildings after the defeat of the Crusades to keep going the piety of following Christ on his way to Golgotha). The memory selectively and creatively maintained by groups is thus a memory of scenarios, of connections between roles. Bastide then turns to Lévi-Strauss and the contrasts he draws between the engineer who acts on formal rules and the *bricoleur*, who assembles odds and ends in a happy-go-lucky manner. Humans can, through specialized training, become engineers but in fact concrete individuals and groups work as *bricoleurs*.

That Bastide promoted an approach to sociology informed by ethnography meant bucking a trend in the world of French scholarship. We are familiar with the suspicion that since Descartes French minds are addicted to clear and distinct ideas, and to sharp dualistic contrasts (e.g. body/mind).[11] But there is also in French air the weight of the tradition issued from the great adversary of Descartes, Pascal, who maintained that the dignity of humans lies in their ability to think. "Man is but a reed, the weakest in nature, but a thinking reed." Pascal also used the border between France and Spain as a metaphor for the discontinuities inherent in space. To suggest that thought might be conditioned by the facts of embodiment and by the social and historical context was knocking a crown off the head of mankind in general and of university professors in particular. Philosophers and the older school of social scientists could on this point be united in the defence of their contribution to the dignity of man, as it had been traditionally conceived. The dominant "scientific" tradition in the early twentieth century did not believe it possible to learn from savages, even though Montaigne had said just that—and Pascal knew it.

Chapter 11

The aesthetic dimension, or the black hen lays white eggs

> Be a Columbus to whole continents and worlds within you.
>
> H.D. Thoreau, *Walden*

Black and white are colours found in nature in relatively pure condition; think of ebony and ivory. These two contrasted colours have been found universally to be convenient, for cave paintings first, and for identifying the two sides in games that oppose two players, such as chess, checkers or backgammon. They were therefore put to frequent use in all cultures. The sharpness of the contrast also caused the two words to become overlaid with qualitative oppositions: dirty and clean, impure and pure, bad and good. In time the adjectives were used to sharpen the contrast between the colour of people's skins. The pink-beige tone of some became labelled "white" and the darker tones of others "black." Once used to designate what came to be called races, the originally innocent and perceptually helpful contrast between the two colours served to justify oppression and crimes, by offering an apparently natural legitimation.[1]

The process illustrates a common bent of language: to carve out distinct realities, to spread clear ideas, to essentialize and substantialize. These processes lay the ground for sharpening of differences, and can henceforth serve as grounds of all-out oppositions and total wars. Adjectives and nouns are particularly liable to such distortions.[2] No such extreme contrasts are found in nature, if perceived with an innocent eye. As the folk poet in Rio put it: black hens lay white eggs.[3] From these eggs, I might add, hatch yellow chickens, which in time turn black and start laying white eggs. Bastide also quoted the poem telling of the Whites who dirty their clothes while the Black washerwomen make them white. The symbolic equivalencies of the two adjectives are inverted. "Your destiny is to make white everything that the White man blackens."[4] The social scientist notes the social impact of such poetry. Nishida refers to the data from the 1976 national census: the Brazilian population found "136 colour labels for self-description." There is obviously no room for sharp contrast among all the shades.[5]

The argument of this chapter is that the aesthetic dimension of life is the best resource the mind has for overcoming the tendancy to see contrasts as final.

In *The Story of Lynx,* Claude Lévi-Strauss offers a reflection on dualities in general that bring into clear relief what is involved in the story of hens and eggs. After surveying a large collection of Amerindian tales collected over time in British Columbia, Lévi-Strauss shows that genuine twins are impossible in North American native mythology. They may well be virtually identical at first, but as soon as they lead real lives, they become differentiated. In these tales, bi-partitions fail to establish a stable equilibrium or a stable contrast; there is in each pair a principle of mobile unbalance between the two sides that quickly goes to work. This, he adds, is in clear contrast with the thought patterns present in European stories. Twins are identical and appear to remain so. Or they are absolute enemies. Romulus and Remus remain identical while one is good and the other bad: Founder and Transgressor are brothers and just mirror images of each other.[6] Lévi-Strauss also found the pattern of rapidly differentiating twins in Brazilian native mythology. In the New World, he concludes, intermediate positions keep being constructed between A1 and A2. In the Old World, biblical monotheism and Persian dualism lead to God and the Devil. In the *City of God* Augustine gives separate spiritual descendants to Cain and Abel, in the two great and eternally contrasted companies of the damned and of the saved. So we find in Paul the contrast between slaves and sons, and we see medieval sculptures of blinded synagogue and triumphant church.

Bastide inscribes his work in the New World pattern when he becomes an ethnologist sensitive to differences arising from context, and when he evokes the accounts of Gilberto Freyre. The Portuguese masters keep themselves separate when they find a Portuguese and Catholic wife to produce an heir that will inherit the estate. Yet he and his slaves live daily as part of the same reality, the large patriarchal family. Their common Catholicism left ample room for cultural differentiation and for sexual mixing.[7] Bastide took seriously Freyre's attempt to insert the realities of common and everyday erotic moments into the flow of social time and to assess the durable ramifications. (This inquiry is admittedly more complex than that which produces statistics on orgasms).[8] He also rallied to the view put forward by Gurvitch defining religion as what can stand above all social antinomies and all brutal power relations. He thus could see religion not in the lines drawn to contrast pure Catholics with syncretistic ones (or oppose legitimate marriage to master-slave fornication), but in the series of social constructions that produce hybrid babies and integrate them (to some extent) to the whole. Hybridation thus rises to the status of central social fact. Our civilization took a turn toward exogamy a long time ago; the erotic traffic between *casa grande* and *senzala* is, in its specific and dire circumstances, in line with this preference. The mulatto children do not exactly repeat the lives of their genitors. Non-egalitarian relationships within the patriarchal family can be morally significant. The erotic dimension is perpetuated in the hybrid festivals in which all share and which become an all-embracing social fact. The powerful enforce stable power relations. Force is force. But symbols are mobile and undermine faits accomplis. Looking at territories rather than maps, Bastide finds on the ground countless intermediate shades and no absolute contrast. Bastide found another aphorism in the source that gave him the black hen. The white sheet of paper is worthless, uninteresting; but put a pen with black ink to it and you start having a poem or a drawing.[9]

Since the days of Freyre and Bastide, the work of Louis Dumont showed us the harm done by egalitarian ideologies that claim that A1 and A2 are basically alike. As Paul Lehmann argued, egalitarianism in the United

Bastide on acculturation

In an article entitled "Problems of the Inter-Penetration of Civilizations and their Works", Bastide discusses acculturation, the term he prefers because it points to a dynamic process. After referring to the pioneering work of Redfield, Linton and Herskovits (*American Anthropologist* 38, 1936), he credits Gurvitch with having stressed that culture is a process. Acculturation is the creation of new "works of civilization" under the pressure of new conditions. It results from thousands of micro-processes of imitation, invention, learning and adaptation, in thousands of individuals and groups. What comes from outside a group is first reinterpreted in the light of the available mental world. When a stronger exterior power breaks up the weaker society, individuals are left with the task of carving for themselves new individual attitudes, which may quickly slide into the pathological. Balandier showed that the situation should be thought of in dialectical terms: each of the groups in contact has some form of impact on the others.

In this call for further work, Bastide invites historians to learn from ethnologists (we do have ethno-history now) and asks for further developing typologies of contacts. Some acculturation is free and spontaneous; some is forced and forcibly organized; there are many intermediate forms. External and internal causalities must always be kept in mind. This is where sociology has a specific contribution to make.

States "is not substantial enough to break the bonds of hierarchy and establish right relationships among human beings." [10] He refers to Dumont's two books *Homo Hierarchicus* and *From Mandeville to Marx*[11] to show the solid link built between ideological egalitarianism and racist social attitudes. When moralistically egalitarian people realise that it is in their interest "to keep Negroes in their place," race dogma is the only way out of their dilemma. "A nation less fervently committed to democracy could probably live happily in a caste system."[12] People, argues Dumont, need to be provided with means to conceptualize differences, and this is what hierarchical systems have always done. When differences are acknowledged, interaction is less blind and patterns of reciprocal relationships stand a chance to see the light of day. Hierarchically ordered relationships place people with unequal powers in relationship with each other. What they do for each other, or with each other, is inevitably asymmetrical. But the absence of equality does not mean that the relationship is necessarily

Asymmetrical or unequal relationships

Readers of Saint Paul find in the Letter to the Ephesians (5:21–6:9) a series of moral exhortations addressed to three kinds of human beings who find themselves placed in a hierarchical relationship, as it were by nature. He addresses wives and husbands, children and parents, and finally, masters and slaves. Wives are to be subjects to their husbands, children must obey their parents and slaves must be obedient. Husbands are to love their wives, fathers should not provoke their children and masters are to do good to their slaves. Thus, within the unchanging framework of hierarchy, and resulting difference of duties, a moral reciprocity is still established. A second version of these assymetrical duties is found in the Letter to the Colossians (3:18–4:1), where masters are urged to treat their slaves justly and fairly.

Lists of (apparently) intrinsically hierarchical and assymetrical relationships are found in Aristotle, in the Buddhist Sigala Homily and in the most famous treatise of Confucius. With the Chinese sage, the list is extended to emperor and subject and to older and younger brother. Thus Confucius thinks he has established the right order for all human relations. Paul on the other hand limits himself to household matters.

New Testament scholars have pointed out that in the case of Paul (or of the author of the two letters), the exhortation is addressed as well to the inferior members of the hierarchy. They are even addressed to them first. Early Christian originality consists then in treating women, children and slaves also as moral subjects. The quality of the relationship is also entrusted to them. There is even in Ephesians a significant turn of phrase of universal significance for the members of the Christian community; "Be subject to one another out of reverence for Christ." It is also repeated that the superior members are likewise charged with a duty of obedience, this time to God.

proceeding without moral norms. For instance, one commands and protects, the other obeys and is protected.

Another social scientist, Éric Blau, drew attention to the two generic forms of social differentiation: heterogeneity and inequality.[13] Heterogeneity distributes individuals horizontally, in terms of nominal parameters (sex, race, religion, occupation). This establishes non-negotiable differences ("Biology is destiny." "They are just born this way"). Inequality distributes vertically in terms of graduated parameters (income, wealth, education, age) and this establishes the possibility of measurable mobility. The history of Brazilian race relations is characterized by the presence of darker and lighter intermediaries between the two extremes; shades are acknowledged and the lines between "elect" and "damned" weaken. There is a tertium quid between rigid hierarchy and ideological equality. In that middle world, difference becomes, as Lehmann puts it, the opportunity of reciprocity.[14]

Nouns and adjectives tend to interpret A1 and A2 to mean either equality-identity or incorrigible heterogeneity. Fortunately humans ordinarily speak complete sentences, although today much is made of sound bites. Humans can also read entire paragraphs, even whole books—or in very rare cases the entire work published by a major thinker. In such cases, style can begin to correct the nefarious bent of language toward essentialization. Style undermines the bent of language to produce pure and simple truths, because, thanks to sentences and their sequences, thanks to the subtleties of grammar and the dramas of tone, the speaker or writer can interrupt the complicity with the powerful verbal simplification dominant in his or her own tribe. Sentences introduce into discourse the freshness of perception and the dimension of art. Leonardo da Vinci put it succinctly: there are three kinds of people, those who see, those who see when shown, and those who don't see. Aesthetic activity deploys a communicative skill that helps increase the number of those in the second category. Art invents showings that make it possible for more people to see.

It is impossible to think without words, and hard to think with them. But we do manage to think with them. A highly original illustration of the exceptional powers of style is found in the *Cannibal Manifesto* published by the poet Oswald de Andrade in 1928.[15] The work does not fit the canons of rhetorical style: it is a sequence of short, assertive paragraphs, with occasional incomplete sentences. It celebrates the Tupi, the native tribe which, in 1556, captured the shipwrecked Portuguese bishop, Dom Pedro Sardinha, and ate him. Hence the strident affirmation: "I am only interested in what is not mine, the law of all men, the law of the cannibal." The manifesto rejects all catechisms along with all monarchical government.

Subsequent commentators on this manifesto find an omnipresent subtext. The inhabitants of Brazil got on the world stage in 1557 when the German traveller Hans Staden published *True Story and Description of a Country of Wild, Naked, Grim, Man-eating People in the New World.* Written in German, the book became a best-seller in many languages.[16] A further wave of interest started in 1578 when the French traveller Jean de Léry narrated his long sojourn in the Bay of Rio de Janeiro and his fraternizing with the Tupi, who invited him to a victory meal that included enemies on the menu.[17] If Brazil became known as a land of cannibals, de Andrade is obviously of the opinion that, in fact, it is Portugal that ate up Brazil, killed its population and emotionally maimed those that survived. (They were "importers of canned consciences" and halted "dynamic thinking"). In cannibalistic acts, the Europeans appropriated the gold first, then the sugar. Only two Europeans are praised, Freud "who finished off the enigma of woman" and Lévy-Brühl who studied primitive mentality. So the time has come for Brazilians to become cannibals (again) and assimilate what is not theirs, to become carnal, to enjoy women, and indulge in the orgies that the wealth of the land and of its population allows. "Before two Portuguese discovered Brazil, Brazil discovered happiness."[18] To my knowledge, Bastide never refers to this manifesto but he quickly caught the flavour of the São Paulo artistic avant-garde and its rejection of European models. He was fully appreciative of the social activism and anti-colonial revolution built on an aesthetic.

The dispossessed suffer the consequences of the flaws in the dominant thinking. They need poetry and they produce it in their popular culture. Their masters enjoy the good life in their big house and derive cognitive comfort from stable ideology and hackneyed sentences. But, as Diderot showed in *Jacques le Fataliste* (1778; printed 1786), the servants do the daily work of perception and see how brittle is the edifice of stable language. The history of political conflicts, when carefully analysed in all their dimensions, show that militant actors ordinarily draw upon the full range of possibilities that language allows. Modern protesters draw also upon one ideology: they insist on being treated as equals. But, after this opening salvo, they skilfully draw upon the whole symbolic advantages that their cultural differences provide them with. This, in fact, may well be their best weapon. Their weaknesses then can begin to be turned into strengths. In the midst of all the instituted language, their discourse becomes instituting.

De Andrade and other poets have fun with the slipperiness of language and turn the play to their advantage. Bouveresse draws a contrast between two responses to the enduring inadequacies of language. Poets experiment with its oddest features and incongruities; they have fun— and communicate. Philosophers are distressed with the impossibility of ever getting things straight forever. They try to weed out improper uses and pare talk down to reliable knowledge. They develop a technical language —and speak to a small, specialized audience.[19]

Six years after Bastide's death, two younger scholars who were influenced by him, and who have since done much to keep him on the map, prolonged some points found in his literary criticism, by examining as anthropologists the realities of the theatre. (We recall that Bastide saw the importance of the innovations in Brazilian Black theatre). Jean Duvignaud, who wrote a major ethnographic study on a Tunisian village, also published *Le Jeu du jeu,*[20] and Georges Balandier, who has to his credit numerous studies on Black Africa and a *Political Anthropology,* published *Le Pouvoir sur scènes.*[21] On the stage, language very clearly becomes both meaning and action, thanks to a *representation*, namely thanks to a fiction, to a scenario that constructs a sequence of relatively simple roles and situations. Stage drama manages to show that powerful clashes of characters are ultimately conflicts of symbols.

Duvignaud begins his book by rehearsing the statement, familiar since Kant's *Critique of Judgement*, on the disinterested nature of art and play (and games too). Humans are capable of a field of experience detached from any end setting and any ordinary consideration of "real" utility (and efficiency). This is what constitutes *l'imaginaire.* The activity of *l'imaginaire* constructs imitations (carefully or not) and is freely playful. It often thrives on leaving things to luck, thus acting on the assumption that only luck is powerful enough to alter the conditions of the real living experience. In the theatre the imitation is complex (based on a carefully written text) and is performed for a group. A gamble is taking place: the performance may lead to a new and shared insight. The nature of the applause attests the degree of success. After the fifth act, life returns to its ordinary course. At curtain call, lago looks normal, and seems a fine person as he holds hands with the other comedians. There is a keen pleasure in knowing that all the drama is taking place in a magic sort of location, on stage, and that Romeo and Juliet, who are at the end innocent victims of singular bad luck, both die but do not die for good. Nevertherless, even though the play is not for real, the suspension of disbelief makes it as good as real, and the cognitive gains may be durable. The performance of the story, therefore, awful though the end is, embodies a profound rejection of the way families control their adolescents, and suggests that in the great game of life, the cards might be dealt afresh. What then is really real? What exhibits the pattern of life possible tomorrow? The rivalry between the Montagues and the Capulets, or what Romeo and Juliet experience? And on which side is Shakespeare, who completes his play in the way we know?

The realities of such performances have great relevance for students of inter-cultural contacts. Spectators enter into a fiction. As Freud argues, in the theatre "just supposing" enables the spectators to come to terms with things ordinarily repressed in their daily life. In the same way, the ethnologist, by "making as if" he is a member of an Afro-Brazilian group gathered in a *tereiro*, begins a process of inner transformation, for himself and for those who will read him (if he writes well).

Professors of religion do not all go to the theatre or do participant observation. But when they teach, they inevitably become actors. Everybody, being embodied, is visible to others, willingly or unwillingly. Humans have appearances. Humans also shape their appearances and sometime give them (in the strong sense of giving) to a particular other or group of others. Then they offer a spectacle, play a role, and act up, even if only a little. This is even true of those who do their "acting" simply, and sometimes dully, from behind a lectern. From live teaching to good writing there is but a small step. Any reflection on the art of writing raises the question of the involvement of the writer with the reality he is apparently dealing with in a distant manner. Where exactly is the inside of the author who puts black marks on the white screen? Where is the inside of the lecturer who is outside the audience and speaks to it? Likewise, we may ask as to who is inside the culture of Candomblé? The Afro-Brazilian who stages the ceremony before the eyes of welcome visitors and acts it out, or the outsider who is attentive to the ritual taking place in the room where he sits? In all these examples, humans are involved in an aesthetic activity. They process signs.

This brings us to the old problem about the consciousness of the comedians. They act on stage and work on their appearance. But they are part of a plot they did not devise and utter feelingly words that are not theirs but which they make their own in some sense. Desdemona is convincing to the audience but the actress does not change her identity (or does it only temporarily and in some qualified sense). Hence the famous interrogation: what do great actors do? Do they produce an intelligent artifice and control it perfectly, or do they throw themselves into the role and become, for a while, the character imagined by the author? And how big is the difference between the theatrical and the social stage? Diderot, in *Rameau's Nephew*, a text much admired by Hegel, blurred the line very successfully between social comedies and theatrical ones. At the end of the film *Stage Beauty*, Othello/Edward Kynaston (portrayed by Billy Crudup) and Desdemona/Maria (Claire Danes), who interacted actively and significantly in "real" life, perform on stage the final scene of the tragedy in a very powerful way, and rightly earn great applause. Assessing what happened afterward, off-stage, the actor tells the actress: "I killed you, and you did not die." The viewer is left with the conundrum. The author, writes Maurice Blanchot, is like the actor; he is an author only when he writes. Like the comedian, he must let his performance go when he has completed it, and he cannot catch his work again when he has given it to the public.[22]

The point of all this is that the theatre, by stretching the space that exists between the self and itself demonstrates the enduring non-coincidence beween the individual and itself. I submit here that scholarly writers too have a complex relationship to what they put down on paper. They both participate in it and don't participate. The emphasis is on participation when they sign their work. But they may have recourse to irony in their text, use suspension marks, or try to hit the nail with a metaphor. They may add a new paragraph of which readers have trouble to know whether it qualifies the previous one, provides another perspective, or simply challenges what has just been said. It is harder to stop the dialectic than start it. Poets and philosophers explore, in their different ways, the continent of language, the vast interior caverns where differences keep echoing inside the self. The consequence of this is that the good author, like the comedian, does not just think before her readers, or for them, but she gives them something to think about. She leads them to the point where they must cut out their own path, and do their own thinking. In other words, she surrenders her work to the world of exteriorities with which others will do as they please.

In the study of religion, as in all cultural studies, one cannot avoid occupying ground where *l'imaginaire*, that is visions rooted in an imaginative capacity, or presentations of that which is not but might be, flourish and invade consciousness. But the consciousness of the writer and that of the reader never merge—or if they do they do not do it for long. So writers and readers must get into grey areas, live with some *chiaroscuro* halfway between clarity and obscurity. Maria Isaura Pereira de Queiroz praises Bastide for always remaining on the firm ground of actual consciousness. In her view, he practised some auscultation that tried to listen to what is half-hidden, but he never claimed to have defeated some hypothetical censorship that supposedly managed a successful cover up of what is *really* there. Here Bastide does not follow Freud's path.[23] There is a fringe area between the unconscious and the conscious that he is much interested in, but he never attempts to pierce the boundary; he goes no further than what the individual seems half-conscious of.

The same attentiveness to what lies halfway between reality and unreality, and seems to be a mix of both, is relevant to the study of large-scale social and religious phenomena. On this issue it is Balandier's book *Le pouvoir sur scènes* that develops Bastide's insights in the most helpful way. Force, as distinct from violence, can operate only by producing images, argues this anthropologist. (Freyre's slave master needs to have a permanent whipping post). Great heroes always have dramatic effect. In Greece, theory got started by staging conflicts before audiences, in theatres. At the Renaissance, powerful kings organized a vast retinue to stage themselves in more and more elaborate ways. Oppositional power also found new ways of setting "truth" against power—with varying degrees of success. The great contest between order and disorder is always conducted with images, and the flavour of the sacred can appear on either side of the struggle.[24] I should add that Balandier's last pages offer a saddened account of modernity. The cold power of the modern State masters a soft and steady technology of appearances. Order successfully defends itself against derision. Festivals have become entertainment and have lost their intrusive impact on the imagination. The more we see, the better informed we think we are, but the more captured we become. What he calls *theatrocracy* has achieved its monopolistic ambitions.[25]

The religious histories that Bastide wrote about are always seen within the framework of some historical drama. After the Revocation of the Edict of Nantes (1685), the French Protestants had to choose between exile and a clandestine and hunted existence. The rural populations (Bastide's ancestors) stayed in France but were left without ministers; they were comforted by lay prophets who received visions and incited congregations to trances.[26] Transported Africans were robbed of their freedom and collective memory and found some freedom by reconstituting a memory and performing rituals. The first book written by Bastide on the Candomblé put it this way: the vitality of the cults rests on the fact that it moves from mysticism to aesthetics.[27] Urbanized Afro-Brazilians adapted to the competitive life required in their society ostensibly committed to egalitarian principles. Bastide's pupils wrote on the *cangaceiros*, the heroic "bandits of honour" who are celebrated in folk art, greatest among them being the illustrious Lampião who transformed the anger of starving people in the Northeast into some organized capture of wealth from those who have it.[28] Or they wrote on the messianic leaders who started a holy sort of war.[29] The twilight zones of the imaginary cannot be kept out of the visible, public histories. Here also Bastide kept his feet on the ground, but the ground is rough, not smooth, as are complex and divided all the people standing on it. Here again the question cannot be eluded: what is the author's relationship to what he signs? One of Bastide's African pupils in Paris recalled discussing Marx with him. He stated that Bastide came right out—he never was a communist and never would be, but he was a *gauchiste*. One can see here an echo of the statement of the nineteenth century socialist Proudhon to the effect that syntheses are always oppressive and on the government's side.[30]

So there is a homology between the scholar-writer, the ethnographer moving to another continent, the sociologist attentive to acculturation and the writer who is sensitive to the power of literature. In each aspect of his work, Bastide locates himself in the interval, in the intermediate area. When people speak, they place words in the middle between them. Ignorance and knowledge co-exist in the middle. Live human beings are always in-between realities in which they participate; they embody a mixture and carry on with mixtures of being and non-being.[31] Bastide recalled that Margaret Mead invited James Baldwin to think about their common ancestry—an indubitable fact, provided one goes back far enough. Bastide, supported by Freyre, looked carefully at the Brazilian proclivity for giving birth to mixed race bastards (two terms that in English struggle to find value-free equivalents), and he carefully considered the consequences of the practice. *Mestiçagem* becomes in his work a metaphor for both living and thinking.

Bastide, who tried his hand at writing poetry and who published his very first articles on literary matters, was still very much alert to questions of art at the end of his life. In 1970 he wrote a long preface to one of the last fictions of Jorge Amado, *A morte e a morte de Quicas Berro Dagua* and drew attention to the aesthetics of this piece of literature. He admits the relevance of the view Gilberto Freyre presents of the duality between the grandeur of the mansion and the squalor of slave quarters to the work of many modern Brazilian novelists and poets. Is there an intimate relation between misery and poetry? Such a dialectic relationship is found in a distinguished literary French source, namely Victor Hugo, who shocked readers by taking them into the lower rungs of society, to scenes of human misery and crime. This Romantic poet undertook to turn around French classical aesthetics by showing the beautiful in the ugly, the high in the low. There are some forms of human greatness and nobility that are found only among the poor and distressed. It takes the work of artists to bring it all to life—and public visibility. Amado, scion of a land-owning family, wrote poetically of the lives of the people of Bahia, people who were very different from the ones he knew in his family and in his Jesuit school. Like Hugo he made it apparent that *misery* and *poetry* should not be thought as being in a substantial opposition but in a mutually enriching relationship. It is by exploiting this vein, transgressing the social limitations inherited from his class and acculturating to Afro-Brazilian life that Amado became a great writer.[32] Sitcoms can be written about the life in the great houses of the owners of plantations. There is deeper stuff awaiting the perceptive artist in the quarters of the slaves—although it remains true that the life of the poor has also been often sentimentalized.

Bastide's last book, *L'anatomie d'André Gide* (1972), is also on problems of aesthetics.[33] At the beginning of his own career, Gide, an artist who gave the impression he was never faithful to himself, wrote a play (*Saül*, 1903) on the first Hebrew king. This countryman whose she-asses escaped, went into the desert to look for them. But there, in the place of lonely desolation, he got a big surprise. He met with the prophet Samuel who told him that the people had asked for a king and that God had chosen him for this rank, and that he would anoint him as such.[34] Saul of course forgot about the she-asses. Gide and Bastide always took for granted that the best things in life do not come by effort; they are not like the objects people set their minds on and look for. There is gratuitousness ahead of all. (She-asses can be forgotten and it is permitted to do gratuitous acts). The story of Saul also has a dark side: the old king lost the favour of God and of the people, as the fame of young David spread. David never ceased to recognize the legitimacy of Saul, but kingship became hollow as the old man ceased being loved and admired. Nothing is ever final in human life—except death. Gide and Bastide believe people should not turn to Saint Anthony of Padua to help them find their lost she-asses; they should take their losses and move on to new and unforeseeable opportunities. (As a matter of fact, Saul incurred the divine wrath when he turned to a witch to gain insight into his future).

And at the end of his life, Gide wrote *Thésée* (1946), a fictitious account of his own life given by the old king of Athens. Theseus went to Crete to defeat the Minotaur. He got the help of Ariadne, daughter of the king there, who gave him the thread that enabled him, after slaying the monster, to find his way out of the labyrinth and fall into the welcoming arms of the princess. But then, later, the hero abandoned Ariadne on an island, and moved on. Her thread had become a chain hobbling his feet. (He thus solved his own princely masculine problem of possessing without being possessed). All his life Gide feared getting trapped and affirmed that humans are what they become. Admitting his homosexuality and acting on it liberated him from the constraints of his acquired Protestant moral rigidities. Some literary contemporaries applauded. Most Protestants were not amused. (Today we would point out that, as he pursued his therapy in North Africa, he did not verify the age of his consenting partners). Bastide kept a deep sense of the inevitability of disorder in human affairs. He expressed it with a metaphor from the topography of his native Cévennes mountains. There is a rich chaos below all the maps of the surveyors, and we must keep the innocence of the look that sees beyond and below the boundary stones. But we do have surveys and boundaries—and we keep repairing them. We have The Law and we need it. We are however ambivalent about laws. This is why we both reform them and play beyond their limits.

Gide allowed one sort of pride to Theseus: to have built the city of Athens. I venture that this is an achievement Bastide himself considered to be a very high one—and probably the sort of achievement that motivated his interest in acculturation and his tireless action on the intercultural scene. Before the "Court of International Opinion", assembled to consider the "Case of City Building," the expert Bastide presented two fully documented exhibits. Exhibit A showed the recreation of culture in the Americas in general, but mainly in Brazil, by transported African slaves, who, through their construction of a religion, became able again to steer their own boats, in spite of the evil winds. Exhibit B examined the extent to which the multi-level realities of hybridation contributed in one nation state to the elaboration of a common future for a society made up of people with very diverse pasts. An intellectual biography seems the appropriate way to present his work. In the world of the schools he was a sociologist and this made it possible for him to build a scientific discourse. But the biographies of the human beings he tried to understand remained at the centre of his concerns. He could feel that his own memories and anticipations overlapped somewhat with theirs. So his scholarly work is part of his attempt to rise to the challenges imposed to his generation, in his lifetime. As is the case with most authors of some depth, his thought cannot be properly understood without some understanding of the drama of his life.[35]

Notes

Chapter 1

1. Full bibliographic information on Bastide's books, articles, prefaces and book reviews is found in *Bastidiana* 3 (1993, reprinted 1997) 3–94. The same issue also gives (95 ff.) a bibliography of 450 texts on Bastide.

Chapter 2

1. Outside of France, the names of Freud and James Joyce come to mind.
2. See Gérard Namer, "Postface" to Maurice Halbwachs, *Les cadres sociaux de la mémoire* (1994 [1925]), 300–304.
3. In 1896 the poet Fréderic Mistral opened his museum in the city of Arles, as a depository of provençal life and culture. He wrote his verses in the regional language and this was the swan song of the long and distinguished tradition of provençal poetry. The founding of the Arles Museum is the most visible turn to the conservation and praise of regional folklore, a movement accompanied by a shift in politics from monarchism to right-wing republicanism and the collapse of militant Catholic politics. See Lebovics (1992).
4. He does not mention the confessional difference since the ethos of the French public school did not allow drawing attention to communitarian differences. Protestants and Jews were particularly careful on ignoring the topic.
5. "Discours de distribution des prix, Lorient, 1926," Bastidiana 19/20 (1997), 18–19.
6. "Le sacré sauvage" in *Le sacré sauvage et autres essais* (1975). The Geneva conference published under the title *Le besoin religieux* (Neuchâtel: La Baconnière, 1973) includes the discussion that followed.

Chapter 3

1. A positivist wing of psychology worked on the physiological basis of behavior, with forays into the neurological, while another studied character. Both were very attentive to the abnormal—and both were pre-Freudian.

2. To call Frank Abauzit a translator is somewhat misleading since he produced an adaptation. The French reading public still does not have a proper translation.
3. Pickering (1994), 343–359.
4. Richard, *La femme dans l'histoire,* (1909).
5. Quoted in Lukes (1973), n.314.
6. Quoted in Lukes (1973), 415.
7. Translated in Pickering, (1994), 228–276.
8. Camille Tarot, *De Durkheim à Mauss, l'invention du symbolique. Sociologie et science des religions,* (1999), 340–341.
9. Richard published a posthumous biography of Allier: *La vie et l'oeuvre de Raoul Allier* (1948). It focuses mainly on his career in the French Reformed Church. While his youthful interest in psychology of religion was part and parcel of his protestant intellectual family, his mature pieces on the subject are quite free from confessional flavors.
10. First edition 1931; reprinted in Paris 1996. English translation, London, 1934.
11. His corpus is thus almost exclusively Christian, but he uses the work of Massignon on Muslim saints.
12. *Grande Revue,* (1931), reprinted in *Le sacré sauvage* (1975), 13–25.
13. *Grande Revue,* (1934), reprinted in *Le sacré sauvage* (1975), 39–69.
14. Reprinted 1947.
15. On Durkheim, Camille Tarot (1999, 263) makes a very penetrating comment:

    > If he systematically privileges the ethnography rather than the history of religion, it it not only because the ethnology of the day promises and promotes the primitive, it is also because it is (and this greatly simplifies the task) a sociology without language, speaking of primitives whose discourse does not count or is insignificant (my translation).

16. Translated by Mary Baker; foreword by James L. Peacock (2003).
17. The role of Durkheim in the Affair is discussed in Lukes (1973), 330–354. Fur the full text of "Individualism and the intellectuals" see Pickering (1994), 59–73.
18. Lukes, chapter 21, "The sociology of morality" (1973), 410–436.
19. This is the main thrust of the critical analysis Gurvitch (1963, 175–202) makes of Durkheim's view of mores and morality.
20. Lukes (1973), 500, see also 428.
21. Pickering (1994), 354.
22. Reprinted 1994, with an afterword by Gérard Namer.
23. Halbwachs (1893, revised 1902, translated 1933).
24. Halbwachs (1994), 231–232, 266–267.

25. Halbwachs (1994), 244, 263. See also the comment of Gérad Namer in his Postscript, 366.
26. Halbwachs (1994), 268. De Tocqueville found that in the 1830s New York was more civilized than Paris because different professional classes met more freely in their social life.
27. Halbwachs (1994), 253–265. Comment by Namer (2000), 363–366.
28. Halbwachs died in Buchenwald in 1945; His late papers were published posthumously under the title *La mémoire collective* (critical edition Paris, Albin Michel, 1998). He develops the distinction between collective memory maintained in a group and social memory that endures without linkage to any particular group. See Gérard Namer (2000), *Halbwachs et la mémoire sociale*.
29. Desroche, *The Sociology of Hope* (1979). To-day Danièle Hervieux-Léger sees a privileged relation between religion and memory in *La religion pour mémoire*.
30. Tarot, *Sociologie et anthropologie de Marcel Mauss,* (2003), 24.
31. Mauss (1968), 145–279. *Essai sur le don,* dans *Sociologie et anthropologie*. English translation *The Gift.*
32. Jacques T. Godbout, with the collaboration of Alain Caillé, *L'esprit du don* (2000 [1992]). English translation *The World of the Gift* (1999) also reviews the literature on giving in post-traditional societies.
33. Mauss (1968), 273–279.
34. Camille Tarot, *De Durkheim à Mauss, l'invention du symbolique: Sociologie et science des religions* (1999) is a monumental study of the turn to theorizing on symbols which enable sociology to pay much more attention to this diversity of historical religions than was ever attempted by Durkheim. On Mauss, see Tarot (2003) *Sociologie et anthropologie de Marcel Mauss*.
35. See introduction by Nathan Schlanger to M. Mauss, *Techniques, Technology and Civilization* (2006), 22.
36. Schlanger (2006), 10.
37. The left suffered a big loss in the 1919 elections; the unions lost also in a big way in the 1920 strikes. This led to a crisis at its Congrès de Tours in December 1920. The majority of delegates swung to Leninist or Bolshevik revolutionary views—and became the nucleus of the Communist Party. The minority remained reformist and committed to working through the universal (male) suffrage and became the nucleus of the socialist party.
38. Bastide was elected in the municipal election in Cahors in 1924 on the socialist ticket.
39. On the first one he wrote a book late in his life, on the others a few early articles.
40. Gide (1999), 121–126.

41. Queiroz, Maria Isaura Pereira de, (1994, 147–148).
42. These inquiries are published in the review *Christianisme social*, a journal founded by theologically liberal Protestants concerned with social justice, Élie Gounelle being most visible among them. See *Bastidiana* 25/26 (1999), *Sociologie et protestantisme*.
43. 1932; reprinted in Bastide, *Le sacré sauvage et autres essais* (1975), 26–38.
44. See Balandier (1972). Balandier calls him "the theoretician of praxis" and credits him with "a sociology of liberty" and "an anti-technocratic alternative."
45. Published in Portuguese in São Paulo. French translation in *Bastidiana* 35/36 (2001), 69–95, *Sociologie de la connaissance*.
46. See James (1943) *Essays on Radival Empiricism and* Wild (1969) *The Radical Empiricism of William James*.
47. The reception of Max Weber in France was notoriously slow. The first significant study is that of Raymond Aron, *La sociologie allemande contemporaine* in 1935. The two essays on the vocation of the scholar and the politician *Le savant et la politique*, were translated in 1959 and *The Protestant Ethic and the Spirit of Capitalism* in 1964.
48. Gurvitch (1963), 325–430.
49. The mature result in Gurvitch (2001 [1966]) *Les cadres sociaux de la connaissance*. English translation, *The Social Frameworks of Knowledge* (1971).
50. See chapter 6, "Le deuxième durkheimisme et la sociologie de la connaissance" in Gérard Namer, *Halbwachs et la morale sociale* (1994), 82–96.

Chapter 4

1. *Les religions africaines au Brésil* (1995 [1960]), 20.
2. "Sociologie du théâtre nègre brésilien" (undated), appendix in *La Candomblé de Bahia* (2000), 388–406.
3. The social picture, with an economic analysis and history of political awakening, is told by Josué de Castro (1966), *Death in the Northeast*. Short indications are available on the beginning of the involvement of the Catholic clergy in support of dispossessed.
4. Amado's political views led him to prison and exile. He left the party in 1956. The world of the popular literature and Candomblé is most effectively evoked in his novel *Jubiaba* ([1936] 1984).
5. Préface of Jorge Amado, *Les deux morts de Quinquin-la-Flotte* (1980), 7–50.
6. "Roger Bastide, pionnier d'une esthétique sociologique" in *Art et Société* (1977), 11–17.

7. Parts of it are available in French in *Poètes et dieux. Études afro-brésiliennes* (2002).
8. *Art et société* (1997 [1977]).
9. The epoch-making book of Alfred Gell, *Art and Agency. An anthropological theory* (1998) works with a notion of art objects that includes Polynesian canoe decorations, idols and the art treasures displayed in national museums. Setting aside the notion that art is a matter of meaning and communication, it argues that art is about doing. Art objects "are devices for securing the acquiescence of individuals in the network of intentionalities in which they are enmeshed" (viii). Most noteworthy also is Gell's definition of anthropology, arguing that it attains its depth of focus by working within a biographical time-frame. Social agents have a time-perspective on themselves, their own lifetime and anthropology distinguishes itself as a discipline by replicating it. In contrast, sociology is often supra-biographical and cognitive psychology infra-biographical .
10. Préface, *Art et société*, (1977), 7–8.
11. Bastide locates his approach to issues of acculturation in the context of previous scientific work in the article "Problèmes de l'entrecroisement des civilisations et de leurs oeuvres" in Georges Gurvitch, *Traité de sociologie* Tome 2 (1960), 315–330.
12. Queiroz, Maria Isaura Pereira de, "Les années brésiliennes de Roger Bastide" in *Bastidiana* 1 (1993), 31–38.
13. Comparison could be made between what the events in Brazil and what happened in Québec in the 1960s, at the time of rapid development of universities and scholarship.
14. Laurent Vidal and Paulo César da Costa Gomes, "Déplacement de savants, déplacement des savoirs. Le glissement des concepts sur le sol meuble du Brésil" in *Bastidiana* 35/36, (2002), 175–181. The authors also inform us that Bastide's first publication in Brésil, an article on the cafuné (a method of killing lice), was greeted with disgust in some circles: do Brazilians need to import Frenchmen to get that sort of science?
15. Queiroz, Maria Isaura Pereira de, (1978), Uma nova interpretaçao do Brasil: a contribuiçao de Roger Bastide à sociologia brasileira, 101–121.
16. http:www.unicaen.fr/lasar/bastidiana/BIO-BIBLIO.html.
17. Bastide, *Les religions africaines au Brésil*, (1995 [1960]), 269.
18. Freyre, *The Masters and the Slaves: A Study of the Development of Brazilian Civilization,* (1956 [1946]).
19. The Church also provided an institutionalized basis for socialization among slaves by recruiting them in a variety of confraternities where the use of the rosary put a varnish of piety over many other things. Bastide, *Les religions africaines*, (1995 [1960]), 66–68, 74.
20. The sociologist Sergio Buarque de Holanda (1902–1982) has described the type of the cordial man.

21. Brazil is on the map of sexual tourism but, unlike some other destinations, government vigilance is high and protection of minors real.
22. Mieko Nishida, *Slavery and Identity. Ethnicity, Gender and Race in Salvador Brazil, 1808–1888*, (2003), 6.
23. Freyre, *The Masters and Slaves,* (1956 [1946]), 321–322, 349–350, 395.
24. Nineteenth century evidence to the contrary is brought forward in Robert Edgar Conrad, *Children of God's Fire. A Documentary History of Black Slavery in Brazil,* (1983), 267–286.
25. Jean Baudrillard, *De la Séduction. L'horizon sacré des apparences,* (1994), 71.
26. Bastide, "La dimension économique" in *Le prochain et le lointain,* (1970), 62–63. Bastide adds that much of the subjective basis of racism is not based on skin pigmentation: fuzzy hair and wide nose are what displeases.
27. Freyre, *The Masters and Slaves,* (1956 [1946]), 278.
28. Bastide translated it (*Maîtres et esclaves*; Paris, Gallimard, 1952 [1946]) and Gurvitch brought an elite of French-speaking sociologists to discuss it at a *Décade de Pontigny.*
29. Comparisons have been made between the condition of the slaves in the cotton plantation of the US with those in the sugar plantation of Brazil. In the past white historians were found on each side to praise the merits of the ways of their nation. In his balanced assessment, Eugene Genovese finds that when it comes to "day-to-day living conditions" US slaves had more food and a higher literacy rate. (They lived in a much more prosperous economy.) But Brazilian slaves had better access to freedom and citizenship. See Eugene D. Genovese (1969), "The treatment of slaves in different countries: problems in the application of the comparative method" in L. Foner and E. D. Genovese (ed.), *Slavery in the New World.* Most assessments tend to forget the frank examination of sexual mores offered by Freyre and his case for a syncretistic quality in mores and culture.

    Albert J. Raboteau (2004) also sketches a comparison in his *Slave Religion. The "Invisible Instiution" in the Antebellum South.* He holds the view that Catholicism was more conducive to the survival of African religion than was Protestantism. This survival was also facilitated by the high mortality rate in Brazil and the continued influx of fresh arrivals.
30. Fernanda Areas Peixoto (2000) wrote an intellectual biography of Bastide, *Dialogos Brasileiros: Uma analise da obra de Roger Bastide*, covering his youth and his years in Brazil. She focusses on his involvment in the artistic and intellectual life, and introduces us to the work of his major interlocutors.

Chapter 5

1. The name of the capital city is Salvador de Bahia, sometimes now

referred to as Bahia. It was the capital of colonial Brazil until 1763 and for a period of time the most populated city in the Americas. It is situated on the Bay of All Saints, *Bahia de todos los santos*, sometimes also called *Bahia de todos los pecados*—this version of course does not appear on maps. See Nishida, *Slavery and Identity*, (2003), 10–17.

2 *Images du Nordest mystique en noir et blanc,* first edition 1978; new edition 1995, witrh a preface by Jean Duvignaud. In the course of doing this work, the French translator found reasons to believe that the translator into Portuguese had worked quickly and made some mistakes. So a team of scholars familiar with the whole of Bastide's work reviewed it to produce what is now considered an authoritative text.

3. In his study of early narratives by French travelers to Brazil, Michel de Certeau (1991, 221–226) alludes to the page where Freud writes of the subconscious insinuating itself through cracks in the sober discourse.

4. In his discussion of the narrative of Jean de Léry's travel to and sojourn in the Bay of Rio de Janeiro (1557–1558), Michel de Certeau (1975, 215–248) discerns the root of the traveler's cognitive distress: these people are very different (they go about naked and eat their enemies killed in battle) but their music and dance make them erotically attractive.

5. Maristela Oliveira de Andrade, "Roger Bastide em viagem ao Nordeste" in *Roger Bastide e o Brasil,* (2004), 79–98.

6. This is the occasion to refute Durkheim's view and his view of a collective mystical experience to explain the social.

7. Bastide gave a full-length article on *Exu*, on his transformations in the journey from Africa to the various sites in the New World where he is attested. "Immigration et métamorphose d'un dieu", in *Le prochain et le lointain,* (1970), 211–226.

8. Leather provides the major income of the great landowners. Areas of concentrated population are too remote for meat to be marketed.

9. On the history and current expansion of the *capoeira,* see Floyd Merrell (2005), *Capoeira and Candomblé: Conformity and Resistance through Afro-Brazilian Ezperience.*

10. *Bastidiana* 45/46 (2004) reprints fourteen minor texts on Candomblé accompanied by twelve articles on the topic.

11. *Le Candomblé de Bahia (Rite Nago)* Paris-La Haye, Mouton, 1958.
In 2002, the book was reprinted (Paris, Plon) in the well-known collection *Terre humaine.* This publishing event is turned into a celebration of the work of Bastide. The book received illustrations, indices, a selective bibliography of the works of Bastide, and an appendix of four reprinted articles. There are also numerous introductions, first among them that by Fernando Henrique Cardoso, President of the Republic of Brazil, who recalls his days as Bastide's student. He credits Bastide with having introduced him to all the classics and with teaching him fieldwork—his

teacher sent him to do a report on an asylum for the insane. He also celebrates Bastide's enormous culture. Jean Duvignaud stresses the importance of the 1944 trip and the recaptured innocence of the look; he traces this ability back to Bastide's background in France. Jean Malaurie, the director of the collection, deplores that it took so long for Bastide to get the readers he deserved. There is also a text by Duvignaud previously published in *Le Monde des Livres* in 1995.

In 2000 Claude Ravelet wrote a reception study, *Roger Bastide. De la disgrâce à la renaissance* (*Bastidiana, Hors-série* 6) seeking to explain the apparent oblivion into which Bastide's work fell after his death in 1974 and the rebirth in the 1990s, starting with the Colloque of Cerisy in 1992.

12. E. Franklin Frazier, the sociologist who opened up the field of sociological study of US Blacks promptly condemned the "Africanism" of Herskovits and defended his view that Blacks in the US kept nothing of their African past.
13. As we shall see, Bastide stresses that these cults are a novel creation.
14. See Marcel Griaule, *Arts of the African Native* (1950) and *Conversation with Ogotemmeli*, the unfolding of a cosmology (1965).
15. Recent work on Yoruba rituals considers the process rather than the structure and focuses on the agency of the practitioners. See the book by Margaret Thompson Drewal (1992), a specialist of performance studies, *Yoruba Ritual: Performers, Play, Agency;* also Mikelle Smith Omari-Tunkara (2005), *Manipulating the Sacred: Yoruba art, ritual and resistance in Brazilian Candomblé*.
16. D. Cuche, "Le concept de principe de coupure et son évolution dans la pensée de Roger Bastide," in *Roger Bastide ou la réjouissement de l'abîme,* (1994), 69–83.
17. Reprinted 1995, with a preface by Georges Balandier, "Une sociologie de la rencontre." English translation by Helen Sebba, *The African religions of Brazil: toward a sociology of the intepenetration of civilizations* (1978). Gurvitch had encouraged Bastide to prepare the dissertation during his visit in São Paulo. Note that his two major works are published respectively four and six years after his arrival in Paris.
18. The first two are sociologists or social theorists, the third one is a psychologist and the last is the towering figure in the history of philosophy.
19. William James is now credited with a refutation of foundational empiricism. As Richard Rorty (2004, 86–97) now puts it, there is no such thing as an intrinsic content of experience. In other words, experience does not dictate the language in which it is described. It is however unwise to let our lives be dominated by concepts and commands that make no contact with experience.
20. Bastide, "La dimension religieuse," *Le prochain et le lointain,* (1970), 47–48, 100–102. Bastide refers to the case of the gifted child of a slave woman who was sent to Montpellier to study medicine in the eighteenth

century.

21. A distinction is to be made between the coastline where the Jesuits have influence and the world of the plantations where the chaplains feel the authority of the master. Catholic principles would lead all to oppose the erotic dances, but the masters want to encourage a good reproduction rate among their slaves. In the hinterland, the visits of the priests are rare and the catholic cult rests upon the good will and zeal of the population. See "L'acculturation folklorique" in Bastide, *Le prochain et le lointain,* (1970), 164–168.
22. Bastide, "La dimension sexuelle. Vénus noires et Apollons noirs" in *La prochain et le lointain,* (1970), 77–87. Eroticism cannot be understood apart from social factors.
23. Bastide adds an allusion to Piaget's work on the formation of moral sentiments in children.
24. Bastide found a mixture of black and white magic in the *umbanda* and stated "religion" was falling apart in that movement. From his somewhat brief notations, authors showed that there was more coherence in the sect and that Bastide voiced the views of an Africanist prone to see a norm in the world of Candomblé. See David J. Hess, "Umbanda and Quimbanda magic in Brazil: Rethinking aspects of Bastide's work," *Archives de sciences sociales des religions* 79, (1992), 135–153. Hess adds that Bastide's work became a sort of Scripture and that his pages on Candomblé are referred to by some as the orthodoxy.
25. Roberto Motta revisited the work of Bastide on the urban transformations of Candomblé in Southern Brazil and updates the research on these groups in "L'expansion et la réinvention des religions afro-brésiliennes: réenchantement et décomposition," *Archives de sciences sociales des religions* 117 (2002), 113–125.
26. See the contrast drawn between the Catholic Christianity of Incarnation and the Protestant one of Death and Resurrection in "La causalité externe et causalité interne dans l'explication sociologique," *Bastidiana* 66 (2001), 35–36.
27. See Cristian Parker (1996), *Popular Religion and Modernization in Latin America. A Different Logic* and André Corten (1999), *Alchimie politique du miracle. Discours de la guérison divine et langue politique en Amérique latine.*
28. "Introduction," *Poètes et dieux. Études afro-brésiliennes* (2002).
29. Sahlins (2000), Chapter 1, in *Culture and Practice. Selected Essays* III.

Chapter 6

1. *Bastidiana* 33/34 (2001) reprints eight texts by Bastide on African topics.
2. *African Cvilizations in the New World,* with a foreword by Geoffrey Parrinder (1971).

3. Vol. I, 65–82.
4. Vol. II, 315–330.
5. Vol. II, 402–420.
6. J. Poirier ed. *Ethnologie générale,* 1037–1090.
7. "L'état actuel de la recherche en sociologie religieuse." In H. Desroche and J. Séguy (eds.), *Introduction aux sciences humaines des religions,* (1970), 129–144.
8. "Les cultes afro-américains." In *Histoire des religions,* vol. 3, (1976), 1027–1050.
9. Jean Duvignaud. "Vingt-cinq siècles d'ethnologie." *Magazine littéraire* 167, December (1980), 8–13. Syyed Hossein Nasr (1968) has documented the wealth of ethnographic work done by medieval Muslims in his book *Science and Civilization in Islam.*
10. Pioneering work was done by Victor Segalen (1878–1919), a navy doctor who arrived in Polynesia in the course of his duties and stayed. He wrote *Les Immémoriaux* (1907), a novel on a Maori priest who has lost "the ancient language."
11. Introduction, *Le prochain et le lointain,* (1970), 10–11.
12. Paris, 1967.
13. In Guy Hunter, ed., *Industrialization and Race Relations* (1965).
14. *Le prochain et le lointain*, (1970), 55–75.
15. *Le prochain et le lointain*, (1970), 123–134.
16. *Le racisme en question* (1972).
17. "Introduction", *Poètes et dieux*, 11–12. He adds that the same attentive ear led him to say the things that were not obvious in France about the Protestantism of Gide or the Jewishness of Proust.
18. Maria Isaura Pereira de Queiroz (1994, 147–167) summarizes the account Bastide gives of this series of authors and what their works indicate about the social situation of Afro-Brazilians.

Chapter 7

1. French translation, with a preface by Roberto Motta, *Poètes et dieux. Études afro-brésiliennes* (2002).
2. These three books offer a limited sample of Bastide's scattered articles. A further thirteen of them are reprinted under the designation anthropology of religion in *Bastidiana* 42/43 (2003) 17–210. Another thirteen of them are reprinted under the designation Philosophie et sociologie in *Bastidiana* 47/48 (2004).
3. *Significations* (1986), 2.
4. *Le prochain et le lointain*, (1970), 89–122.

5. Jeremiah 18; these verses are echoed in Saint Paul's letter to the Romans (chapter 9, v. 19–24).
6. "Le folklore brésilien," *Le prochain et le lointain*, (1970), 157–189.
7. This is also the conclusion of the classic study by Maria Isaura Pereira de Queiroz of the 1912–1916 movement know as the *Contestado* in the Southern Province of Santa Catarina. See *La guerre sainte au Brésil. Le mouvement messianique du Contestado* (1957).
8. 'Mythes et utopies," *Le prochain et le lointain,* (1970), 247–257
9. While there are no polemics, the whole of Bastide's work amounts to a refutation of Eliade's work. See the pages in *Le Candomblé de Bahia* (2000, 295, 305) where he shows how the contingencies of history and its conflicts spelled out the death of metaphysics. He concludes that it is not the rise of logical thought but this cultural transformation which is at the origin of modernity.
10. The phrase is taken from Roland Barthes.
11. Bastide refers here to the work of Roger Caillois, *Le mythe et l'homme* (1938) and also to Roland Barthes, *Mythologies* (1957) and his account of modern mythologies as alternatives to political expression.
12. Anthony F.C. Wallace, *The Death and Rebirth of the Seneca* (1969); P. Worsley, *The Trumpet Shall Sound: A Study of Cargo Cults in Melanesia* (1957).
13. Vittorio Lanternari, *The Religion of the Oppressed* (1963).
14. Primitive societies are not conscious of the possibility of change through concerted or resolute effort. See *Les cadres sociaux de la connaissaance,* (1959), 37. Modern societies exhibit a promethean tendency toward having overly sanguine expectations about what "effort" can achieve.
15. The story of Louis Riel, the Métis leader hanged in Saskatoon in 1885, shows a similar type of messianism in French Canada. More modestly, all he prophesied was the transfer of the See of Saint Peter to Saint Boniface Manitoba.
16. *Le rêve, la transe et la folie,* (1972), 30.
17. Note 1, *Le rêve, la transe et la folie,* (1972), 45.
18. In Candomblé every person in a trance is shadowed by a sister who knows how to calm, hold and comfort if the need arises.
19. The sociology of the theatre was explored by one of his pupils, Jean Duvignaud; *L'acteur. Esquisse d'une scoiologie du comédien* (1965), *Sociologie du théâtre. Essai sur les ombres collectives* (1965), *Spectacle et société* (1970). At the same time, Lucien Goldmann, a Marxist, wrote *Pour une sociologie du roman* (1964).
20. "Rencontres de cvilisations et maladies mentales," in *Le rêve, la transe, la folie,* (1972), 229–241.

21. *Le Rêve, la transe et la folie,* (1972), 243.
22. "Des fausses fenêtres ou de la symétrie dans la pensée morbide", *Le rêve, la transe, la folie*, 243. Delirious thinking keeps painting false windows on the façade to multiply artificial symmetries and have a view of reality more reassuring that the reality itself. Delirium is just an extension of the defensive character of culture.
23. Harding (2000), 151–153.
24. Such ideas were voiced by Marcel Mauss as early as his 1902–1903 *Esquisse d'une théorie générale de la magie* in *Sociologie et anthropologie,* 3–131). Translated as *A General Theory of Magic* (1972).
25. Caetano Veloso, quoted in Floyd John Merrell, *Capoeira and Candomblé. Conformity and Reistance in Brazil* (2005), 289.
26. The fertile influence of his writings on a variety of contemporary social scientists is evidenced by two recent international conferences. One was held in Recife in 2004; its proceedings are printed in *Bastidiana* 49/50 (2005); this issue also reprints five texts of Bastide. The other was held in Caen and Anduze in 2005; proceedings in *Bastidiana* 51/52 (2005) and 53/54 (2006).
27. *Philosophical Investigations*, 2nd edition, reprinted English only 1978.

Chapter 8

1. See the preface by Ricardo Motta to *Poètes et dieux.*
2. "Bastide mas all de los cultos afro," In Marisella Oliveira de Andrade (ed.), *Roger Bastide e o Brasil*, 23–38.
3. The distance is a bit less than half that between Saint Malo and Québec, Plymouth and Massachusetts, or Seville and Cartagena.
4. *Os Nago e a mporte. Pade, Asese e o culto Egun na Bahia* (1984 [1872]).
5. This view of the new analytical tools is much indebted to J. Lorand Matory, *Black Atlantic religion,* (2005).
6. See Serge Gruzinski, *Mestizo Mind: the intellectual dynamics of colonization and globalization* (2002). Most of the examples are draw from Hispanic America.
7. *Force of circumstance,* (1968), 523–537.
8. Police harassment was commonly justified by accusations of illegal practise of medicine.
9. Ruth Landes, *The City of Women,* (1994 [1947]).
10. Robert A. Voeks, Sacred *Leaves of Candomblé. African Magic, Medicine and Religion in Brazil,* (1997).
11. Paul Christopher Johnson (2002), *Secrets, Gossip and Gods: The Transformation of Brazilian Candomblé.*

12. Floyd Merrell (2005), *Capoeira and Candomblé: Conformity and Resistance in Brazil.*
13. Matory, *Black Atlantic Religion,* (2005), 220–223.
14. On routes, travel and "practices of displacement", see Part One of James Clifford, *Routes. Travel and Translation in the Late Twentieth Century,* (1997). See also Richard C. Folz, *Religions of the Silk Road. Trade and Cultural Exchange from Antiquity to the 15th Century,* (1999).

Chapter 9

1. *Elementary Forms of the Religious Life*, 64. Quoted in Steven Lukes, *Émile Durkheim*, (1973), 24. Lukes adds (26–28) very damaging criticisms. The sacred-profane bi-partition derives from the basic dichotomy between the social and the individual, is too rigid and static and does not allow for situational flexibility.
2. *Elementary Forms,* 62.
3. Rudolf Otto (1958 [1923]), *The Idea of the Holy. An Inquiry into the non-rational factors in the idea of the divine and its relation to the rational.*
4. Otto gives currency to the notion of a religious *a priori*. The category of the holy is transcendental, i.e. a universal condition of possibility of all religious experience.
5. Roger Caillois, *Man and the Sacred,* (1960 [1938]).
6. On this group see the texts collected by Denis Hollier (1979), with a brief introduction, in *Le Collège de sociologie*.
7. Georges Bataille, *Théorie de la religion* (1973), translated as *Theory of Religion* (1989).
8. Mircea Eliade, *The Sacred and the Profane: The Nature of Religion,* (1959).
9. Alphonse Dupront, *Du Sacré. Croisades et pélerinages. Images et langages,* (1987).
10. *Le sacré sauvage,* (1975), 234. An important 1937 article "Le chrétien et l'organisation sociale," in *La Revue du christianisme social*, August (1937, 35) further elaborates on this point.

    One can add here that Bastide's reluctance to try to understand what happened between Moses and God is also related to his preference for work on egalitarian religious movements, rather like the one he was raised in, because in them language is shared and not just received. Religious hierarchies are seen as a threat, since the support they give to the faithful is tainted by their need to maintain their power.
11. Terror management theory traces the ramifications of the fact that humans, unlike other animals, know that their death is inevitable. Cultures thus get viewed as symbolic protectors.
12. *Le sacré sauvage,* (1973), 215, 217.

13. The contrast between the past and the present participles is a constant feature in the thought of Bergson. See Bastide's review of *Les deux sources de la morale et de la religion* in "Le sacré sauvage," (1973), 77–80. It has also been used to account for tension in the theology of the New Testament. See J.-L. Leuba (1950), *L'institution et l'événement. Les deux modes de l'oeuvre de Dieu selon le Nouveau Testament. Leur différence, leur unité.*
14. Those who find their overarching concern in the business of living together will profit from the study of the process philosophy put forward by Charles Sanders Pierce. Religionists then might well study "signing" rather than signs. The sentences of Floyd Merrell may require being read twice, but they make the point neatly. "There is no signing and hence no meaning without culturing, that is, contextualizing. Culturing involves permanent signing processing; signing processing cannot genuinely emerge without living; and living depends on signing processing agents interminably interpreting their world. Indeed, cultural processing enters into a liquid embrace with meaning-interpreting processing." *Processing Cultural Meaning* (2007, v).
15. "Mémoire collective et sociologie du bricolage" in *Année sociologique* 21 (1970), 107. Reprinted in *Bastidiana* 7/8 (1994), 209–242.
16. Henri Desroche, Introduction to *Sociology of Hope,* (1979).
17. Georges Gurvitch, *Les cadres sociaux de la connaissance,* (2001), 41.
18. "Les cadres sociaux de l'anthropologie culturelle américaine", *Cahiers internationaux de sociologie,* January 26, (1959), 15–26.
19. Françoise Morin, "Les inédits et la correspondance de Roger Bastide" (1994), 24.
20. *Phénoménologie du sacré. Essai sur l'anthropologie culturelle de Roger Bastide*, dissertation EHESS 1978.
21. *La rêve, la transe, la folie,* (1978), 39.
22. Henri Desroche (1974), *Les religions de contrebande. Essais sur les phénomènes religieux en époques critiques.*

    His pupil Maria Isaura Pereira de Queiroz inserted the history of a Brazilian messianic movement in the world-wide history of such messianisms. *La guerre sainte au Brésil* was originally a thesis directed by Bastide.
23. *Anthropologie appliquée,* 182–183, 205–207.
24. M. Mauss, "Rapports rééls et pratique de la pychologie et de la sociologie," *Sociologie et anthropologie* (1950, 306–308).
25. One could draw a contrast between Bastide and Bataille, who, raised a Catholic, celebrates the eros (or lust) for melting into the mountain-hole. The young Bastide opposed Catholic mystics who swoon to the Protestants who imitate Christ ("Mysticisme et protestantisme," *Bastidiana* 25/26 (1999) 11–14). Jean Duvignaud states the contrast thus: in the sixteenth century Western

Europe got split between two metaphysical visions: there were those who celebrate expense and those who celebrate economy. *Le Jeu du jeu* (1980, 215).

26. The ethnologist of the Tupi Gurani (an indigenous tribe now living in both Paraguay and Brazil) Hélène Clastres has a nice phrase; "to be mortal and to be social are two sides of the same coin." *La terre sans mal. Le prophétisme tupi-guarani* (1975, 124)
27. Baudelaire, *Petits poèmes en prose*, no. 33.
28. Claude Lévi-Strauss, *La potière jalouse* (1988), 229; *The Jealous Potter*; *Histoire de lynx*, (1995), 251–253; *The Story of Lynx*.
29. Maurice Leenhardt criticized Lévi-Strauss in a 1965 article "La pensée obscure et confuse" (in *Le monde non-chrétien*). Bastide discussed the confrontation; "Conclusion d'un débat récent: la pensée obscure et confuse" in *Bastdiana* 2 (1993). See also the discussion in James Clifford *Person and Myth* (1992), 78–180.
30. "Roger Bastide. Les lointains et les ânesses," *Bastidiana* 4 (1993), 67–74.
31. "Conférence sur les phénomènes de la participation," *Archives des Sciences Sociales de la Coopération et du Développement* 51, 1980.
32. Bastide, *African civilizations in the New World* (1971), 75.
33. Gurvitch defined the task of sociology as the study of freedom as it meets obstacles. In recent US scholarship, the anthropologist Marshall Sahlins has most consistently advanced the view that culture is the work of diversified freedoms. *Culture and Practical Reason* (1976) argues that humans live according to a "meaningful scheme of their own devising," and that meaning derives from a symbolic structure that attends to more than material utility. The second volume of *Culture in Practice* defines culture as imagined totality devised to make life bearable, the sum total of efforts made to avoid being miserable. It wrenches human from what is simply given to get fresh air from the "land of the possible."
34. Gurvitch, *Les Cadres sociaux de la connaissance*, (2001 [1966]), 57–62.
35. Gurvitch, *La Vocation actuelle de la sociologie*. Vol II, *Antécédents et perspectives* (1963), 325–430.
36. N. Schlanger, Introduction, in M. Mauss, *Techniques, Technology and Civilization* (2006), 25–27.

Chapter 10

1. Pierre Bourdieu (2000), *Pascalian Meditations*.
2. What intellectuals thus cultivate, says Bourdieu, is scholastic reason. All its fallacies are based on the universalizing of a particular case (49). He reminds us also of the page in *Theaetetus* where Plato contrast those

who are in a hurry to make their point and those who can talk at their leisure in peace (13). In ordinary life, time is in short supply.

3. Pierre Bourdieu, *Pascalian Meditations*, (2000), 16.
4. The point here is not that the scholar should tell about his childhood experiences but should situate his scholarship in the context of his formative studies. Bruce Lincoln made the point succinctly. "Scholarship is myth with footnotes." It is self-critical, born of discussion and subject to discussion. See "Epilogue: Scholarship as Myth" in *Theorizing Myth: Narrative, Ideology and Scholarship* (1999), 209.
5. The case of empathy is very well summarized by Russell T. McCutcheon in *The Insider/Outsider Problem in the Study of Religion* (1999), 1–11.
6. The contemporary grammar of belief is ambiguous. Depending on the tone, "I believe" may mean I don't know and serve to convey doubt, or can express firm assurance.
7. See R. Needham, *Language, Belief and Experience* (1972), 106–108.
8. See Mary Jo Neitz, "Studying Religion in the Eighties," in *Symbolic Interaction and Cultural Studies*, edited by Howard S. Becker and Michal M. McCall (1990), 90–118.
9. The depth of the processes set in motion is rendered visible in Norbert Elias, *The Civilizing Process* (1978).
10. *L'année sociologique* 21 (1970), 65–108. Reprinted in *Bastidiana* 7/8 (1994), 209–242.
11. Maurice Leenhardt made it his object to introduce obscure and confused ideas in science; "La pensée obscure et confuse" in *Le monde non-chrétien* (1965); see the discussion in James Clifford, *Person and Myth*, (1992), 178–180.

Chapter 11

1. The appropriation of the colour contrast by Brazilian people with darker skins shows a wide range of attitudes. In the culture of the sugar plantations, the white master and mistress are often construed by Blacks as benevolent and the white children always treated with affection. The Black wet-nurse loves her black and white children equally. It is the *feitor*, the foreman, who is conceived to be the fount of cruelty. In erotic phantasms, white women are viewed as desirous of black lovers. In some rare cases of revolt, white women were raped and lynched by their slaves. In nineteenth century Afro-Brazilian educated poetry, white (women, lilies, snow) is used as symbol of purity. "Introduction à l'étude de quelques complexes afro-brésiliens," in *Le rêve, la transe, la folie,* (1972), 203–213.
2. See chapter 8 "The tyranny of taxonomy" in Bruce Lincoln (1989), *Discourse and the Construction of Society: Comparative Studies of Myth,*

Ritual and Classification. See also chapter 9, "The dialectics of symbolic inversion." The book is a fine demonstration that accounts of religious language slant it either toward maintenance or toward resistance and innovation.

3. In the 1840s, Victor Schoelcher, the French abolitionist, had to inform his audiences that African men do not produce black sperm.
4. "Mémoire collective et sociologie du bricolage," (1994), 74.
5. Mieko Nishida, *Slavery and Identity*, (2003), 7, 154. Most of the terms are of course untranslatable in English. There has been in the recent past a series of short-lived political movements of the Black Power type. Nishida suggests that in Brazil blackness is perhaps "perceivable only to those who seek to see it."
6. Claude Lévi-Strauss, *The Story of Lynx*, chapters 5 and 19.
7. *Les religions africaines au Brésil,* (1995), 93.
8. Ten articles by Bastide on sexuality are reprinted in Bastidiana 27/28 (1999) 21–120. Most noteworthy is "Comportement sexuel et religion," 31–48. See also Jean-Pierre Le Bouler "Roger Bastide et l'érotologie de Georges Bataille" in *Bastidiana* 53/54 (2006), 61–76.
9. *Le rêve, la transe et la folie,* (1972), 217.
10. Paul Lehmann, *The Decalogue and the Human Future* (1995), 11.
11. Louis Dumont, *Homo Hierarchicus: The Caste System and its Implications* (1970); *From Mandeville to Marx: The Genesis and Triumph of Economic Ideology* (1977).
12. Here Dumont quotes from Gunnar Myrdal, *An American Dilemma*.
13. Éric Blau, *Inequality and Heterogeneity: A Primitive Theory of Social Structure* (1977).
14. Paul Lehmann, *The Decalogue and the Human Future* (1995), 47. Lehmann finds in Luther, who was still close to the patriarchal world, a greater sensibility to the perils of egalitarian individualism.
15. English translation in http://www.sibila.com.br/slbyl36manifanthropo.html. De Andrade got one fact wrong: Dom Sardinha, the first bishop of Brazil, was eaten by the Caete Indians.
16. French translation, *Nus, féroces et anthropophages* (2005). See also Donald W. Forsyth, "Three Cheers for Hans Staden: The Case for Brazilian Cannibalism." *Ethnohistory* 32(1), (1985), 17–36, and Neil L. Whitehed, "Hans Staden and the Cultural Politics of Cannibalism," *Hispanic American Histoircal Review* 80(4), (2000), 721–751.
17. Jean de Léry, *Histoire d'un voyage en Terre de Brésil* (1994). This edition includes an interview with Claude Lévi-Strauss. Montaigne meditated on this text in one of his most famous essays (I, 31) "On cannibals."
18. The Cannibal Manifesto has been usefully compared with the equally petulant and affirmative *Refus Global* published in 1948 by the Québec

painter Paul Émile Borduas. See Chapter One in Licia Soares de Souza, *Utopies américaines au Québec et au Brésil* (2004).

19. Jacques Bouveresse, "Langage ordinaire et philosophie," in *La parole malheureuse: De l'alchimie linguistique à la grammmaire philosophique* (1971), 347–348. The contrast between a jolly and a gloomy response to the human condition is as old as the Greeks who spoke of Democritus, the philosopher who always laughed and of Heraclitus who always wept. For Montaigne the contrast results from divergent responses to the scantiness of knowledge. "De Democritus et Heraclitus" *Essais* I, 50.
20. Jean Duvignaud, *Le Jeu du jeu* (1980). Duvignaud began writing on the sociology of art and artists in 1967 with *Sociologie de l'art.*
21. Georges Balandier, *Le Pouvoir sur scènes,* (1980); revised expanded edition (2006).
22. Maurice Blanchot, *Après coup* (1983), 86.
23. Queiroz, Maria Isaura Pereira de, "Pour atteindre l'imaginaire," (1994), 164–165.
24. *Le pouvoir sur scènes* (1980). Whenever possible, readers should consult the revised 2006 edition.
25. Balandier returned to these themes in 2005: *Le grand dérangement*: change has become continuous, and completion of process or achievement cannot any more be identified.
26. Aubert Rabenoro, "Le protestantisme de Roger Bastide" *Bastidiana* 25/26, (1999), 137–151.
27. *Images du Nordeste* (1995), 276–277.
28. Queiroz, Maria Isaura Pereira de, *Os Cangaceiros. Les bandits d'honneur brésiliens* (1968).
29. *Le pouvoir sur scène* (1980), 140–141. See Queiroz, Maria Isaura Pereira de, *La guerre sainte au Brésil: le mouvement messianique du Contestado* (1957).
30. "L'apport de la sociologie française à la sociologie de la connaissance" *Bastidiana* 35/36, (2001), 18.
31. Plato, *Republic*, 478d-479d.
32. J. Amado, *Les deux morts de Quinquin-la-Flotte*, préface (1980), 7–50.
33. *L'anatomie d'André Gide* (1972).
34. I Samuel, chaps 9 and 10.
35. I use the word drama in its Greek original sense: namely the things that happened to him and the things he did.

Bibliography

Works by Roger Bastide

Books

———. *Les problèmes de la vie mystique.* Paris: PUF, 1996 (1931). Translated by H.F. Kynaston-Snell and David Waring as *Problems of Mystical Life.* London: Jonathan Cape, 1934.

———. *Éléments de sociologie religieuse.* Paris: Colin, 1947 (1935). Translated by Mary Baker as *Social Origins of Religion*, foreword by James L. Peacock. Minneapolis: University of Minnesota Press, 2003.

———. *Imagens de Nordeste mistico em branco et preto.* Rio de Janeiro: O Cruzeiro, 1945. Translated, with foreword by Jean Duvignaud as *Images du Nordest mystique en noir et blanc.* Arles: Actes-Sud, 1995.

———. *Arte e Sociedade.* Portuguese translation by Gilda de Mello e Souza (São Paulo : Martins, 1945. Original text: *Art et société.* Preface by Jean Duvignaud. Paris: Payot, 1977.

———. *Le Candomblé de Bahia (Rite Nago).* Paris: Plon, 2000 (1958).

———. *Les religions africaines au Brésil. Contribution à une sociologie des interpénétrations de civilisation.* Paris: PUF, 1995 (1960), with foreword by Georges Balandier. Translation by Helen Sebba as *The African Religions of Brazil: toward a sociology of the interpenetration of civilizations.* Baltimore, MD: Johns Hopkins University Press, 1978.

———. *Sociologie des maladies mentales.* Paris: Flammarion, 1965. Translated by Jean McNeil as *Sociology of Mental Disorder.* London: Routledge, Kegan Paul, 1972.

———. *Les Amériques noires.* Paris: L'Harmattan, 1996 (1967). Translation by Peter Green as *African civilisations in the New World,* with foreword by Geoffrey Parrinder. New York: Harper and Row, 1971.

———. *Le prochain et le lointain.* Paris: Cujas, 1970.

———. *Anthropologie appliquée.* Paris: Payot, 1971. Translated by Alice L. Morton as *Applied Anthropology.* London: Croom Helm, 1973.

———. *Le racisme en question.* Paris: Calmann-Lévy, 1972.

———. *Le rêve, la transe et la folie,* with a préface de François Laplantine. Paris: Le Seuil, Point-Essais, 2003 (1972).

———. *Anatomie d'André Gide.* Paris, PUF, 1972.

———. *Estudos afro-brasileiros.* São Paulo: Perspective, 1973. Translated with a preface by Roberto Motta, as *Poètes et dieux. Études afro-brésiliennes.* Paris: L'Harmattan, 2002.

———. *Le sacré sauvage et autres essais.* Preface by Henri Desroche. Paris: Payot, 1975.

Articles

———. *Discours de distribution des prix. Lorient* (1926), *Bastidiana* 19/20 (1997),18–19.

———. *Un mysticisme sans dieux. Grande Revue* (1931), 11–112. Reprinted in *Le sacré sauvage*, 13–25. Paris: Payot, 1975.

———. *La plongée ténébreuse. Grande Revue* (1932), 459–470. Reprinted in *Le sacré sauvage, 26–38.*

———. *Dieu et la Révolution. Essai sur les rapports entre l'Église et la démocratie. Grande Revue* (1934), 460–486. Reprinted in *Le sacré sauvage,* 39–69.

———. La causalité externe et la causalité interne dans l'explication sociologique, *Cahiers internationaux de Sociologie*, vol. 21, 1956. Reprinted in *Bastidiana* 35/36 (2001).

———. *Les cadres sociaux de l'anthropologie culturelle américaine. Cahiers internationaux de sociologie January 26, 1959: 15–26.*

———. Problèmes de l'entrecroisement des civilisations et de leurs oeuvres. In George Gurvitch, *Traité de sociologie* II, 315–330. Paris, PUF, 1960.

———. *Sociologie et psychologie.* In G. Gurvitch, *Traité de sociologie,* vol. 2, 65–82. Paris: PUF, 1960.

———. *Sociologie et psychanalyse.* In G. Gurvitch, *Traité de sociologie,* vol. 2, 402–420. Paris: PUF, 1960.

———. *Les effets de l'industrialisation sur les relations raciales au Brésil.* In Guy Hunter (ed.), *Industrialisation and race relations,* 9–29. New York: Oxford University Press, 1965. Reprinted in *Le prochain et le lointain*, 55–76. Paris: CUJAS, 1970.

———. *L'apport de la sociologie française à la sociologie de la connaissance. L'Homme et la Société* 2 (1966), 46–50. Reprinted in *Bastidiana* 35/36 (2001), 11–26.

———. *Préface to Contributions à la sociologie de la connaissance,* 7–12. Paris: Anthropos, 1967.

———. *Mythologie.* In Jean Poirier, (ed.), *Ethnologie générale,* 1037–1090. Paris: Gallimard, 1968.

———. *Psychologie et ethnologie and Psychiatrie sociale et ethnologie.* In Jean Poirier, (ed.), *Ethnologie générale,* 1625–1654. Paris: Gallimard, 1968.

———. *L'état actuel de la recherche en sociologie religieuse.* In H. Desroche and J. Séguy (eds.), *Introduction aux sciences humaines des religions,* 129–144. Paris: Cujas, 1970.

———. *Immigration et métamorphose d'un dieu.* In *Le prochain et le lointain.* Paris: CUJAS, 1970.

———. *Mémoire collective et sociologie du bricolage. Année sociologique* 21 (1970), 65–108. Reprinted in *Bastidiana* 7/8 (1994), 209–242.

———. *Acculturation, Anthropologie religieuse, Initiation, Intériorité et subjectivité, Magie, Religons négro-américaines, Sacrifice, Utopie.* In *Encyclopaedia Universalis,* 1971–1972. Paris.

———. *Les cultes afro-américains.* In *Histoire des Religions,* vol. 3, 1027–1050. Paris: Gallimard, 1976.

———. *Conférence sur les phénomènes de la participation. Communautés: Archives de Sciences Sociales de la Coopération et du Développement* 51 (1980), 6–24.

———. *Conclusion d'un débat récent: la pensée obscure et confuse. Bastidiana* 2 (1993), 77–89.

———. "Mysticisme et protestantisme," *Bastidiana* 25/26 (1999).

———. *Sociologie du théâtre nègre brésilien.* In R. Bastide, *Le Candomblé de Bahia,* 388–406. Paris: Plon, 2000.

———. *La sociologie de Georges Gurvitch. Bastidiana* 35/36 (2001), 69–95.

Works about Roger Bastide

Brumana, Fernando Giobellina. Bastide mas alla de los cultos afro. In Marisella Oliveira de Andrade, ed., *Roger Bastide e o Brasil*, 23–38. Manaira: Religare, 2004.

Cuche, D. Le concept de principe de coupure et son évolution dans la pensée de Roger Bastide. In Philippe Laburthe-Tolra (ed.), *Roger Bastide ou la réjouissement de l'abîme*, 69–83. Paris: L'Harmattan, 1994.

Durand, Gilbert. Les lointains et les ânesses. *Bastidiana* 4 (1993–1994), 67–74.

Hess, David J. Umbanda and Quimbanda magic in Brazil: Rethinking aspects of Bastide's work. *Archives de sciences sociales des religions* 79 (1992), 135–153.

Laburthe-Tolra, Philippe. *Roger Bastide ou le réjouissement de l'abîme.* Paris: L'Harmattan, 1994.

Motta, Roberto, L'expansion et la réinvention des religions afro-brésiliennes: réenchantement et décomposition, *Archive de Sciences sociales des Religions* 47, 117 (2002) 113–126.

Morin, Françoise. R. Bastide ou l'anthropologie des gouffres. *Archives de sciences sociales des religions* 40 (1975), 99–106.

———. Les inédits et la correspondance de Roger Bastide. In Philippe Laburthe-Tolra (ed.), *Roger Bastide ou le réjouissement de l'abîme,* 147–167. Paris: L'Harmattan, 1994.

Peixoto, Fernanda Areas. *Dialogos Brasileiros: Uma analise da obra de Roger Bastide*. São Paulo: Edusp, 2000.

Queiroz, Maria Isaura Pereira de. Roger Bastide, pionnier d'une esthétique sociologique. In *Art et Société,* 11–18. Paris: Payot, 1977.

———. Uma Nova Interpretação do Brasil: a contribuição de Roger Bastide à Sociologia Brasileira, 101–121. Revista do Instituto de Estudos Brasileiros, São Paulo, v. 20, 1978.

———. Les années brésiliennes de Roger Bastide. *Bastidiana* 1 (1993), 31–38.

———. Pour atteindre l'imaginaire: la contribution de Roger Bastide. In Philippe Laburthe-Tolra (ed.), *Roger Bastide ou le réjouissement de l'abîme,* 147–167. Paris: L'Harmattan, 1994

———. ed. *Roger Bastide. Ensaios e Pesquisas*. São Paulo, Centro de Estudos Rurales e Urbanos NAP-CERU, 1994.

Rabenoro, Aubert. Le protestantisme de Roger Bastide. *Bastidiana* 25/26 (1999), 137–151.

Ravelet, Claude. *Roger Bastide. De la disgrâce à la renaissance. Bastidiana*, Hors-série 6 (2000).

———. (ed.). *Études sur Roger Bastide. De l'acculturation à la psychologie sociale*, preface by Jean Duvignaud, Paris: L'Harmattan, 1996.

———. *Phénoménologie du sacré. Essai sur l'anthropologie culturelle de Roger Bastide*. Dissertation EHESS, 1978.

Verger, Pierre, Les multiples activités de Bastide an Afrique. In *Roger Bastide ou le réjouissement de l'abîme,* 43–54. Paris: L'Harmattan, 1994.

Vidal, Laurent and Paulo César da Costa Gomes. Déplacement de savants, déplacement des savoirs. Le glissement des concepts sur le sol meuble du Brésil. *Bastidiana* 35/36 (2002), 175–182.

Works by contemporaries of Roger Bastide

Amado, Jorge. *Cacau.* Rio: Olympio, 1933.

———. *Jubabia.* São Paulo: Martins, 1935. English translation by Margaret A. Neves. New York: Avon, 1984.

———. *Mar morto.* Rio: Olympio, 1936. Translated by G. Rabanas as *Sea of Death.* New Yok: Avon, 1984.

———. *Capitaes de Area.* Rio: Olympio, 1941. *Captains of the Sands*. New York: Avon, 1988.

———. *Terras do sem fim.* São Paulo: Martins, 1943. Translated as *The Violent Land.* New York: Alfred A. Knopf, 1945.

———. *Gabriela, Cravo e Canela.* São: Paulo: Martins, 1945. Translated by L.J. Taylor and W.L. Grossman as Gabriela, *Clove and Cinnamon.* New York: Knopf, 1962.

———. *Morte e a morte de Quinco Berro D'Agua.* São Paulo: Martins, 1961. Translated into French by George Boisvert, with a preface by Roger Bastide as *Les deux morts de Quinquin-la-Flotte.* Paris: Stock, 1980.

———. *Dona Flor e seus dois maridos.* São Paulo: Martins, 1966. Translated by Harriet de Onis as *Dona Flor and her Two Husbands.* New York: Knopf, 1969.

———. *Sumico da santa.* Rio: Recpord, 1988. Translated by G. Rabamas as *The War of the Saints.* New York: Bantam, 1993.

Aron, Raymond. *La Sociologie allemande contemporaine*, Paris: Alcan, 1935. Translated as *German Sociology.* London: Heinemann, 1957.

Balandier, Georges. *Ambiguous Africa. Cultures in Collision.* New York: Pantheon Books, 1966.

———. *Gurvitch.* Oxford: Blackwell, 1972.

———. *Histoires d'autres.* Paris, Stock, 1977.

———. *Political Anthropology.* London: Allen Lane, 1979.

———. *Le détour. Pouvoir et modernité.* Paris: Fayard, 1985.

———. *Le grand dérangement.* Paris: PUF, 2005.

———. *Le Pouvoir sur scènes.* Paris: Balland, 1980. Revised expanded edition, Paris: Fayard, 2006.

Bataille, Georges. *Théorie de la religion.* Paris: Gallimard, 1973. English translation *Theory of Religion.* New York: Zone Books, 1989.

Bendix, Reinhard. *Max Weber. An Intellectual Portrait.* Garden City, NY: Doubleday, 1960.

Caillois, Roger. *L'homme et le sacré.* Paris: PUF, 1939. Translated as *Man and the Sacred.* Glencoe, IL: The Free Press, 1960.

Caillois, Roger. *Le mythe et l'homme.* Paris: Gallimard, 1938.

Clastres, Hélène. *La terre sans mal. Le prophétisme tupi-guarani.* Paris: Éditions du Seuil, 1975.

de Andrade, Oswald. *Cannibal Manifesto.* 1928. English translation available at http://www.sibila.com.br/slbyl36manifanthropo.html.

de Beauvoir, Simone. *Force of circumstance.* London: Penguin, 1968.

de Castro, Josué. *Death in the Northeast.* New York: Random House, 1966.

Desroche, Henri. *Les religions de contrebande: Essais sur les phénomènes religieux en époques critiques.* Tours: Mame, 1974.

———. *The Sociology of Hope.* London: Routledge and Kegan Paul, 1979.

———. *Socialismes et sociologies religieuses.* Paris: Cujas, 1965.

———. *Dieux d'hommes. Dictionnaire des messianismes et millénarismes de l'Ère chrétienne.* Paris: Mouton, 1969.

———. *American Shakers. From neo-Christianity to pre-socialism.* Amherst: University of Massachusets Press, 1971.

———. *Jacob and the Angel. An Essay in Sociology of Religion.* Amherst: University of Massachusets Press, 1973. Translation of *Sociologies religeuses.* Paris: PUF, 1968.

Durkheim, Émile. *De la division du travail social: Étude sur l'organisation des sociétés supérieures.* Paris: Albin Michel, 1902. (1893). Translated by G. Simpson as *Division of Labpor in Society.* New York: Free Press, 1933.

———. *Elementary Forms of the Religious Life.* London: Allen and Unwin, 1915

Duvignaud, Jean. *L'acteur. Esquisse d'une sociologie du comédien.* Paris: Gallimard, 1965.

———. *Sociologie du théâtre. Essai sur les ombres collectives.* Paris: PUF, 1965.

———. *Sociologie de l'art.* Paris: PUF, 1967.

———. *Spectacle et société.* Paris: Denoël-Gonthier, 1970

———. *Le Jeu du jeu.* Paris: Balland, 1980.

———. Vingt cinq siècles d'ethnologie. *Magazine littéraire* 167, décembre 1980, 8–13.

Eliade, Mircea. *The Sacred and the Profane: The Nature of Religion.* New York: Harcourt, Brace, 1959.

Freyre, Gilberto. *The Masters and the Slaves. A Study of the Development of Brazilian Civilization.* New York: Alfred Knopf, 1946 (revised 1956). Translated into French as *Maîtres et esclaves.* Paris: Gallimard, 1952.

Gide, André. *Essais critiques.* Paris: Gallimard, 1999.

———. *Thésée.* Paris: Gallimard, 1946.

Griaule, Marcel. *Arts of the African Native.* London: Thames and Hudson, 1950.

———. *Conversation with Ogotemmeli, the unfolding of a cosmology.* Oxford: Oxford University Press, 1965.

Gurvitch, Georges. *Les cadres sociaux de la connaissance.* Paris: PUF, 2001 (1966). English translation *The Social Frameworks of Knowledge.* Oxford: Blackwell, 1971.

———. La science des faits moraux et la morale théorique chez É. Durkheim. In *La vocation actuelle de la sociologie,* vol. 2, *Antécédents et perspectives.* 2nd edition, 175–202. Paris: PUF, 1963.

———. *La vocation actuelle de la sociologie,* 2 vols. Paris: PUF, 1963.

Halbwachs, Maurice. *La mémoire collective.* Critical edition. Paris: Albin Michel, 1998.

———. *Les cadres sociaux de la mémoire.* Paris: Albin Michel, 1994 (1925).

Holanda, Sergio Buarque de. *Raizes du Brasil.* Rio de Janeiro: J. Olympio, 1948.

Hollier, Denis. *Le Collège de sociologie.* Paris: Gallimard, 1979.

William James. *Essays in Radical Empiricism and A Pluralistic Universe.* New York: Longmans, 1958 (1943).

Landes, Ruth. *The City of Women.* Albuquerque: University of New Mexico Press, 1947.

Lanternari, Vittorio. *The Religion of the Oppressed.* New York: Alfred A. Knopf, 1963.

Leenhardt, Maurice. La pensée obscure et confuse. *Le monde non-chrétien* 75-76 (1966), 137–156.

———. *Do Kamo. La personne et le mythe dans le monde mélanésien.* Paris: Gallimard, 1971 (1947). Translated by Basia Miller Gulati as *Do Kamo: Person and Myth in the Melanesian World.* Chicago, IL: University of Chicago Press, 1979.

Leiris, Michel. *Race and Culture.* Paris: UNESCO, 1951.

———. *Cinq études d'ethnologie.* Paris: Gallimard, 1988 (1969).

Lévi-Strauss, Claude. *Le regard éloigné.* Paris: Plon, 1983.

———. *La potière jalouse.* Paris: Plon, 1988. Translated into English as *The Jealous Potter.* Chicago, IL: University of Chicago Press, 1988.

———. *Histoire de lynx.* Paris: Plon, 1995. Translated into English as *The Story of the Lynx.* Chicago, IL: University of Chicago Press, 1995.

———. Race et culture, Préface. *Le regard éloigné.* Paris: Plon, 1983.

Lévi-Strauss, Claude. *Tristes Tropiques.* New York: Atheneum, 1973.

Lukes, Steven. *Émile Durkheim. His Life and Work: a Historical and Critical Study.* London: Penguin, 1975.

Mauss, Marcel. *Essai sur le don,* dans *Sociologie et anthropologie.* Paris: PUF, 1968.

———. *A General Theory of Magic.* London: Routledge and Kegan Paul, 1972.

———. Rapports rééls et pratique de la pychologie et de la sociologie. In *Sociologie et anthropologie,* 306–308. Paris: PUF, 1950.

———. *The Gift: The form and reason for exchange in archaic studies.* Foreword by Mary Douglas. New York: Routledge, 1990.

———. *The Nature of Sociology.* New York: Durkheim Press and Berghahn Books, 2005.

———. Techniques of the body. In Nathan Schlanger (ed.), *Marcel Mauss: Techniques, Technology and Civilization,* 77–96. Berghan Books, 2006.

———. Rapports rééls et pratiques de la psychologie et de la sociologie (1924). Translated in *Sociology and Psychology Essays.* London: Routledge and Kegan Paul, 1979.

Métraux, Alfred. *Voodoo in Haiti.* New York: Schocken Books, 1972.

Otto, Rudolf. *The Idea of the Holy: An Inquiry into the non-rational factors in the idea of the divine and its relation to the rational.* Oxford: Oxford University Press, 1923.

Queiroz, Maria Isaura Pereira de. *La guerre sainte au Brésil. Le mouvement messianique du Contestado.* São Paulo: Universidade de São Paulo, 1957.

———. *Os Cangaceiros. Les bandits d'honneur brésiliens.* Paris: Juilliard,1968.

Richard, Gaston. *La femme dans l'histoire.* Paris: 1909.

———. *La vie et l'oeuvre de Raoul Allier.* Paris: Berger-Levrault, 1948.

Santos, Juana Elbein Dos. *Os Nago e amporte. Pade, Asese e o culto Egun na Bahia*. PhD thesis Sorbonne, Paris, 1972; Published in Brazil, Petropolis, Vozes, 1984.

Verger, Pierre. *Trade Relations Between the Bight of Benin and Bahia from the 17th to the 19th Century.* Nigeria: Ibadan University Press, 1976.

———. *Dieux d'Afrique.* Paris: P. Hartmann, 1954. Préface de Th. Monod et R. Bastide.

Wallace, Anthony F.C. *The Death and Rebirth of the Seneca*. New York: Alfred A. Knopf, 1969.

Weber, Max. *From Max Weber: Essays in Sociology.* translated, edited, and with an introduction by H.H. Gerth and C. Wright Mills. New York: Oxford University Press, 1958.

———. *The Protestant Ethic and the Spirit of Capitalism.* New York: Scribner's, 1958.

———. *Le savant et la politique.* Introduction by Raymond Aron. Paris: Librairie Plon, 1959.

Worsley, Peter. *The Trumpet Shall Sound. A Study of Cargo Cults in Melanesia.* London: McGibbon and K, 1957.

Current Works

Baudrillard, Jean. *De la Séduction. L'horizon sacré des apparences.* Paris: Denoël, 1994.

Blanchot, Maurice. *Après coup.* Paris: Éditions de Minuit, 1983.

Blau. Éric. *Inrquality and Heterogeneity. A Primitive Theory of Social Structure.* New York: Free Press, 1977.

Bourdieu, Pierre. *Pascalian Meditations.* Cambridge: Polity Press, 2000.

Bouveresse, Jacques. *La Parole malheureuse. De l'alchimie linguistique à la grammaire philosophique.* Paris: Éditions de Minuit, 1971.

———. *Peut-on ne pas croire? Sur la vérité, la croyance et la foi.* Marseille: Agone, 2007.

Burns, E. Bradford. *A History of Brazil,* 2nd ed. New York: Columbia University Press, 1980.

Carruthers, Michael, (ed.). *The Category of the Person. Anthropology, Philosophy, History.* Cambridge: Cambridge University Press, 1985.

Cazeneuve, Jean. *Lucien Lévy-Brühl.* Oxford: Basil Blackwell, 1972. The book includes selections in revised translations.

Clifford, James. *Person and Myth*: *Maurice Leenhardt in the Melanesian World.* Durham, NC: Duke University Press, 1992.

———. *Routes: Travel and Translation in the Late Twentieth Century.* Cambridge, MA: Harvard University Press, 1997.

Conrad, Robert Edgar. *Children of God's Fire: A Documentary History of Black Slavery in Brazil.* Princeton, NJ: Princeton University Press, 1983.

Corten, André. *Alchimie politique du miracle. Discours de la guérison divine et langue politique en Amérique latine.* Montréal: Éditions Balzac, 1999.

De Certeau, Michel. Travel narratives of the French to Brazil: Sixteenth to Eighteenth Centuries. *Representations* 33(1), (1991), 221–226.

———. *L'écriture de l'histoire.* Paris: Gallimard, 1975.

De Léry, Jean. *Histoire d'un voyage en Terre de Brésil.* Paris: Livre de Poche, 1994 (1578).

De Souza, Licia Soares. *Utopies américaines au Québec et au Brésil.* Québec City: Presses de l'Université Laval, 2004.

Despland, Michel. Les sciences religieuses en France 1880–1886; des sciences que l'on pratique mais que l'on n'enseigne pas. In Michel Despland, *Comparatisme et christianisme: Questions d'histoire et de méthode,* 127–163. Paris: L'Harmattan, 2002.

Drewal, Margaret Thompson. *Yoruba Ritual: Performers, Play, Agency.* Bloomington: Indiana University Press, 1992.

Dumont, Louis. *Homo Hierarchicus. The Caste System and its Implications.* Chicago, IL: University of Chicago Press,1970.

———. Une science en devenir. In *Marcel Mauss,* 8–21. Paris: L'Arc, 1990.

Dupront, Alphonse. *Du Sacré: Croisades et pélerinages. Images et langages.* Paris: Gallimard, 1978.

Durkheim, Émile. *Durkheim on Religion,* W.S.F. Pickering (ed.). AAR Texts and Translations. Atlanta, GA: Scholars' Press, 1994.

Elias, Norbert. *The civilizing process.* London, Blackwell, 1978

Folz, Richard C. *Religions of the Silk Road: Trade and Cultural Exchange from Antiquity to the 15th century.* New York: Saint Martin's Press, 1999.

Forsyth, Donald F. Three cheers for Hans Staden: The Case for Brazilian Cannibalism. *Ethnohistory* 32(1) (1985), 17–36.

Gasché, R. L'Échange héliocentrique. In *Marcel Mauss,* 70–84. Paris: L'Arc-Duponchel, 1990.

Gell, Alfred. *Art and Agency: An anthropological theory.* Oxford: Clarendon Press, 1998.

Genovese, Eugene D. The treatment of slaves in different countries: problems in the application of the comparative method. In L. Foner and E.D. Genovese (ed.), *Slavery in the New World,* 202–210. Englewood Cliffs, NJ: Prentice Hall, 1969.

Godbout, Jacques T., with the collaboration of Alain Caillé. *L'esprit du don.* Paris: La Découverte, 2000. *The World of the Gift.* Montréal: McGill-Queens University Press, 1999.

Goldmann, Lucien. *Pour une sociologie du roman.* Paris: Gallimard, 1964.

Gruzinski, Serge. *Mestizo Mind: the intellectual dynamics of colonization and globalization.* New York: Routledge, 2002.

Harding, Rachel E. *A Refuge in Thunder. Candomblé and Alternative Spaces of Blackness*. Bloomington: Indiana University Press, 2000.

Hervieu-Léger, Danièle. *La religion pour mémoire.* Paris: Cerf, 1993.

Hollier, Denis. *Le Collège de sociologie*. Paris: Gallimard, 1979.

Hunter, Guy (ed.). *Industrialization and race relations. Oxford:* Oxford University Press, 1965.

Johnson, Paul Christopher. *Secrets, Gossip and Gods: The Transformation of Brazilian Candomblé*. New York: Oxford University Press, 2005.

Lebovics, Herman. *True France. The Wars over Cultural Identity 1900–1945.* Ithaca, NY: Cornell University Press, 1992.

Lehmann, Paul. *The Decalogue and the Human Future.* Grand Rapids, MI: Eerdmans, 1995.

Leopold, Anita Maria and Jeppe Sinding Jensen. eds. *Syncretism in Religion: A Reader.* Critical Categories in the Study of Religion. New York: Routledge, 2004.

Leuba, Jean-Louis. *L'institution et l'événement. Les deux modes de l'oeuvre de Dieu selon le Nouveau Testament. Leur différence, leur unité.* Neuchâtel: Delachaux et Niestlé, 1950.

Lincoln, Bruce. *Discourse and the Construction of Society. Comparative Studies of Myth, Ritual and Classification.* New York: Oxford University Press, 1989.

———. *Theorizing Myth: Narrative, Ideology and Scholarship.* Chicago, IL: University of Chicago Press, 1999.

Long, Charles. *Significations.* Minneapolis, MN: Fortress Press, 1986.

Lukes, Steven. *Émile Durkheim. His Life and Work: a Historical and Critical Study.* Harmondsworth: Penguin Books, 1973.

Matory, J. Lorand. *Black Atlantic religion. Tradition, Transnationalism, and Matriarchy in the Afro-Brazilian Candomblé.* Princeton, NJ: Princeton University Press, 2005.

McCutcheon, Russell T. *The Insider/Outsider Problem in the Study of Religion.* London: Cassel, 1999.

Merrell, Floyd. *Capoeira and Candomblé: Conformity and Resistance in Brazil.* Princeton, NJ: Markus Wiener, 2005.

———. *Processing Cultural Meaning.* Ottawa: Legas Publishing, 2007.

Nasr, Syyed Hossein. *Science and civilization in Islam.* Cambridge, MA: Harvard University Press, 1968.

Namer, Gérard. Postscript to Maurice Halbwachs, *Les cadres sociaux de la mémoire,* 297–367. Paris: Albin Michel, 1994.

———. *Halbwachs et la mémoire sociale*. Paris: L'Harmattan, 2000.

Needham, Rodney. *Language, Belief and Experience*. Chicago, IL: University of Chicago Press, 1972.

Neitz, Mary Jo. Studying Religion in the Eighties. In Howard S. Becker and Michal M. McCall (eds.), *Symbolic Interaction and Cultural Studies*, 90–118. Chicago, IL: University of Chicago Press, 1990.

Nishida, Mieko. *Slavery and Identity. Ethnicity, Gender and Race in Salvador, Brazil, 1808–1888.* Bloomington and Indianapolis: Indiana University Press, 2003.

Omari-Tunkara, Mikelle Smith. *Manipulating the Sacred: Yoruba art, ritual and resistance in Brazilian Candomblé.* Detroit, MI: Wayne State University Press, 2005.

Parker, Cristian G., *Popular Religion and Modernization in Latin America: A Different Logic.* Maryknoll, NY: Orbis Books, 1996.

Pickering, William. A note on the life of Gaston Richard and certain aspects of his work. In *Durkheim on Religion*, American Academy of Religion Texts and Translations 6 (1994), 343–359.

Poulat, Émile and Claude Ravelet dir. *Henri Desroche, un passeur de frontières.* Paris: L'Harmattan, 1997.

Raboteau, Albert J. *Slave Religion: The "Invisible Institution" in the Antebellum South.* New York: Oxford University Press, 2004.

Rorty, Richard. Some inconsistencies in James *Varieties.* In Wayne Proudfoot (ed.), *William James and a Science of Religion,* 60–97. New York: Columbia University Press, 2004.

Sahlins, Marshall. *Culture and Practice: Selected Essays* III. New York: Urzone, 2000.

———. *Culture and Practical Reason.* Chicago, IL: University of Chicago Press, 1976.

Schlanger, Nathan (ed.). Introduction. Technological Commitments: Maqrcel Mauss and the Study of Techniques in the French Social Sciences. In *Marcel Mauss: Techniques, Technology and Civilization,* 1–30. London: Berghan, 2006.

Staden, Hans, *Nus, féroces et anthropophages.* Paris: Métaillé, 2005.

Tarot, Camille. *De Durkheim à Mauss, l'invention du symbolique. Sociologie et science des religions.* Paris: La Découverte, 1999.

———. *Sociologie et anthropologie de Marcel Mauss.* Paris: La Découverte, 2003.

Taylor, Eugene and Robert Wozniack. *Pure Experience: The Response to William James.* Bristol: Thoemmes Press, 1996.

Voeks, Robert A. *Sacred Leaves of Candomblé. African Magic, Medicine and Religion in Brazil.* Austin, University of Texas Press, 1997.

Whitehed, Neil L. Hans Staden and the Cultural Politics of Cannibalism. *Hispanic American Histoircal Review* 80(4). (2000), 721–751.

Wild, John. *The Radical Empiricism of William James.* Garden City, NY: Doubleday, 1969.

Wittgenstein, Ludwig. *Philosophical Investigations*. Oxford: B. Blackwell, 1978.

Index

B

C

M

S

T

U

V

W

X

Y

Z

9781845533663.